SIGN LANGUAGE
For
EVERYONE

SIGN LANGUAGE For EVERYONE

A Basic Course in Communication
with the Deaf

by
Cathy Rice

NELSON BOOKS
A Division of Thomas Nelson Publishers
Since 1798

www.thomasnelson.com

Copyright © 1977 by The Bill Rice Ranch

Nelson Books titles may be purchased in bulk for educational, business, fundraising, or sales promotional use. For information, please email SpecialMarkets@ThomasNelson.com.

Published in Nashville, Tennessee, by Thomas Nelson, Inc.

Printed in the United States of America

05 06 07 08 09 10 VG 35 34 33 32 31 30

Library of Congress Cataloging in Publication Data

Rice, Cathy
  Sign language for everyone

  Includes index.
  1. Sign Language. I. Title
HV2474.R48   001.56 77-14592
ISBN 0-8407-9002-3 (hc)
ISBN 0-7852-6986-X (sc)

Contents

Foreword

Tragedy was the catalyst that first prompted Cathy Rice to notice both the need of the deaf and the need for others to learn their language. After a high fever resulting from spinal meningitis left her daughter completely without hearing, Cathy Rice was a young mother with a big burden. In those days in the late 1930s, there was virtually no awareness of the Deaf World.

This especially troubled Bill and Cathy Rice in light of their calling. Bill Rice was an evangelist who traveled extensively, preaching the gospel to thousands who had never heard it. Ironically, neither had his own daughter heard it. Despite the Rices' burden to tell the world the good news, their own child would never "hear" the gospel if someone did not communicate it to her in a way she could understand.

This led the Rices to search for a ministry to the deaf that could help them teach their daughter. Their search was fruitless. Few were even aware there was a need. It began to dawn on them that if Betty was going to understand the Bible, they would need to be the ones to teach her.

Cathy didn't know sign language, but she did know that something had to be done. With the aid of a chalkboard and pictures, Cathy began a daily and deliberate effort to teach her daughter the story of Jesus. After much prayer and hundreds of these lessons, Betty Rice understood her need of salvation and God's provision through His Son, Jesus Christ. Betty trusted Christ when she was eight years old. She was to become the first of literally thousands of deaf persons who would be touched by the life and work of Cathy Rice.

As word of Cathy's class spread to other burdened yet helpless parents of deaf children, Cathy began to receive requests. "Could my son join your class?" "Do you think my daughter could sit in on some of your lessons?" Before long, the Rices found themselves at the forefront of a pioneer effort that had been essentially thrust upon them by personal need. It was a ministry that was tiny but growing.

Bill Rice was quickly becoming aware that their need was not unique. As he traveled the country, he found that for the most part, churches reflected the general ignorance about the deaf that was exhibited by the world at large. This growing conviction led to the realization that God had given them an opportunity and a responsibility.

In 1950, Bill Rice was preaching in a revival campaign in Murfreesboro, Tennessee, just south of Nashville. A realtor who was a member of the sponsoring church told the Rices about a large ranch several miles south of town. Having grown up around horses as a boy in Texas, Bill Rice could envision a ranch retreat where deaf young people could come to ride horses, enjoy camp activities, and learn the Bible. The Rices purchased the place and spent the next three years clearing brush, building, and planning for the arrival of the deaf young people who would be their guests free of charge. What began with twelve deaf campers in 1953 has become a ministry to both the deaf and the hearing, young and old, that has reached multiplied thousands throughout this country.

In the years since, Bill Rice Ranch has produced scores of booklets, lessons, and videos for the deaf and for those involved in deaf ministry. Literally hundreds of churches have begun ministries for the deaf as a result of the ranch's outreach. And many hundreds of people in this country and abroad have learned sign language as a result of the annual Bill Rice Ranch Sign Language School started by Cathy Rice.

Sign Language for Everyone is the result of this school and decades of teaching sign language in a simple, time-tested manner. A clear explanation and illustration with every sign in this book will help you learn and remember both the reason for the sign and how to perform it. It is our prayer that these lessons will increase your interest and your skill as you learn to communicate with the deaf.

Wil Rice IV

President, Bill Rice Ranch, Inc.

Introduction

For the deaf person, understanding those in the hearing world and being understood by others is a never-ending struggle in a world of those, who, for the most part, cannot "speak" their language. By learning the language of the deaf, one can only begin to understand their frustrations and their perceptions of the world in which they live.

This book is designed to teach Sign Language to those who want to understand and communicate in the deaf world. The first seven lessons give instructions for interpreting simple words into signs; the remaining lessons cover, among other things, the differences between English and Sign Language. To avoid confusion, you should study the keys to the explanations for making the signs, and you may also want to review the last five lessons before learning the individual signs.

However, before beginning any of the lessons, it is important to understand a few facts about the deaf.

The deaf are not dumb or mentally deficient.

In speaking of the deaf it is improper to use the term "deaf and dumb." The original meaning of the word "dumb" was "cannot speak." But words do have a way of changing meaning and this word "dumb" has done just that. Today the word "dumb" means "stupid." The deaf are not stupid. Therefore, the word "dumb" should not be used when speaking of deaf people.

The deaf are not mute.

"Mute" means "silent." The fact that a person cannot hear does not necessarily mean he cannot speak. Through these many years in our association with the deaf, we have come across only one boy we thought perhaps mute. But we found that when he was frightened he had a good strong voice.

The deaf lack the ability to use their voices simply because they cannot hear how to use them. Any part of the body not used becomes stiff and unusable. So it is with the deaf person's voice. The deaf need to be taught how to use their voices.

All deaf can be taught to speak.

Some deaf people speak a great deal, others only little. But all can be taught to speak some.

Often parents are led to believe that teaching their deaf child to speak will make him perfectly normal. But in spite of what many educators say, deaf children need special education. Deafness is a handicap.

The greatest need of the deaf is language.

The deaf person needs to be taught the proper use of the English language in reading, writing, and speaking. Every means possible should be employed to help the deaf person grasp a better understanding of the written word. Teaching the deaf child is a difficult task because much of our language is acquired through hearing. Parents should be eager for all methods to be used in conveying this all-important need of language skills to their child. Speech, speech reading, fingerspelling, signs, written language, and hearing aids are among the methods which should be used to train the young deaf child.

Deafness places a person in complete silence; this affects him physically, emotionally, educationally, socially, spiritually, and economically.

Since parents, loved ones, and friends cannot understand him, the deaf person becomes frustrated, lives in a world of his own, and often acts rather queerly. Many times he is placed in a mental hospital. This is unnecessary, however, when those close to the deaf person learn to communicate with him.

In order for a deaf person to learn, someone must have the time and patience to teach him.

The deaf person knows only what someone has taken time to tell him.

We learn much in an accidental way in our everyday routine associations. I am reminded of this often in my daily contact with deaf people.

I remember being in a revival meeting with my husband. Deaf were in the services nightly. One night a man stood to sing a beautiful hymn. I interpreted as he sang. When he finished, I signed to the deaf, "That man has a beautiful high voice."

There was one lovely little deaf woman who had attended the services nightly; she had been married thirty-one years and had been attending church for a long time. When I made the statement about the man's voice, this little woman looked puzzled and asked, "Is that man's voice different from other men's?" It was surprising that a woman her age did not know voices are different. I took time to explain the differences among voices. I told her, as well as the other deaf present, that our voices are all different, just as our faces are different.

I recall the time when our daughter Betty had just graduated from the Tennessee State School for the Deaf. One day I asked Betty to go to the dime store for me.

"Dime store? What's that?"

It startled me at first to think that a twenty-one-year-old girl would not know the term "dime store," but I promptly recovered and came back with, "You know, the store where you buy bobby pins."

"Oh," she said, "you mean the Five and Ten Cent Store!"

Here again, I was reminded that Betty did not know the meaning of "dime store" because no one had taken time to tell her. She could see "Five and Ten" on the store's sign, but she had never seen the word "dime store" written.

There are different means of educating the deaf.

There are several schools of thought regarding deaf education.

The *manual method* teaches by fingerspelling and use of the Sign Language. This method was brought to the United States in the early 1800s by Rev. Thomas H. Gallaudet. Gallaudet became interested in deaf children while in New England, and so he decided to go to England to learn English Sign Language. When he arrived in England he was not treated very cordially. However, while there, he met Abbe Sicard who invited him to visit the French schools for deaf children. He accepted the invitation and consequently spent many months learning the French methods of teaching deaf children.

After his return, Gallaudet opened a school for the deaf in Hartford,

Connecticut, in which he taught the so-called "French method" of Sign Language. This is the language used today in America and around the world.

The *oral method* involves teaching the deaf child to lip-read and to speak to the best of his ability. This method was initiated in the United States by Alexander Graham Bell. He felt that deaf children should be taught to use their voices as much as possible as well as to lip-read as many words as they could. However, Bell intended oral training to be used in conjunction with signs and fingerspelling. His idea was not that of the pure oralists today who say the deaf should never sign nor fingerspell.

The *simultaneous method* uses a combination of all methods—fingerspelling, lipreading, speaking, and signs. This method seems to be by far the most promising and the greatest help to the deaf community.

For many years the oral method was the most emphasized means of teaching deaf children. Parents want to believe the promise, *"Teach your deaf child to speak and lip-read, and he will be just like a normal child."* But lipreading is far more difficult than most people seem to realize. Probably not one in a thousand orally taught deaf can understand all that is said via the lips. Many words look alike on the lips. "Man" and "mat." "Can't" and "call." "You" and "do." "Me" and "be," and hundreds of others. Two incidents involving our deaf daughter will serve to illustrate this point.

For many years, in our town the Ford dealer's name was Binford. My deaf daughter, who is married and the mother of four, was writing a check one day and asked me how to spell "Binford." I spelled, "B-i-n-f-o-r-d," and she asked me if it were a capital "F." I told her it was all one word. For the first time she realized that Binford was one word, not two—Ben Ford. On the lips it looked as if it were two words.

Similarly, for years we talked about a preacher in our town named "Medlock" who we referred to as "Brother Medlock." How surprised Betty was one day when she saw the name written as two words. She had always thought it was one—"brothermedlock."

Many words are formed in the throat and simply cannot be seen on the lips—"come," "carry," "call," "get," and many others. In spite of all this, parents usually prefer their child be taught the oral method.

Parents often feel people will laugh if their child uses Sign Language. At first we felt this way about Betty, but when she was about twelve years old we discovered they laughed at her voice and her attempts to speak. It was then we realized Sign Language and spelling were by far the best means of communication for her. Now we encourage her to speak only with those who know and understand her handicap.

Sign Language is beautiful.

Sign Language is a beautiful and expressive language of natural signs. I always had the idea that the language used by the deaf was just a wild slinging of the arms, but now that I know the language and know the reasons for most of the signs, I realize what a truly beautiful language it is.

No matter how hard we try, it is almost impossible to keep the deaf from signing. While a child is still at home the parents can forbid and punish the child for signing; in oral schools teachers can make the child keep his hands behind his back. But once a deaf person gets out on his own he will naturally revert to signing.

You will often find that many deaf are sloppy and lazy in their use of signs. This is partly because they are not taught proper signing in school. However, there are some deaf people who sign gracefully and beautifully, just as there are people with beautiful speaking voices who enunciate more clearly than others. Also, there are deaf people who seem to have a special talent for "singing"; they can make a song come to life as they gracefully sign the song with rhythm.

We all sign.

All of us use signs a great deal more than we realize. We gesture to get our point across and we use vigorous motions when we are angry.

Babies understand signs long before they understand spoken words. A mother says to her baby, "Come to me." As she says these words she usually puts out her hands and motions for the baby to come. It is the motioning that the baby first obeys, rather than the spoken word.

If you have ever traveled in a foreign country you probably have found yourself using signs. Through Sign Language you can communicate your wants and needs.

Deaf people are happy when we know signs.

Deaf people live in a world of loneliness. Many of them have said to me, "How come you know signs—you can hear?" I always explain I have a deaf daughter, and that is why I learned the language of the deaf. Often they reply, "Yes, but my mother doesn't know signs!"

Deaf people take everything literally.

It is hard for the deaf to understand slang or plays on words. Many words in the Bible such as "thine," "thou," "thee," and "behold" are foreign to deaf people. It is very difficult for deaf people to understand jokes. It is difficult for them to understand such expressions as "sick as a horse," "worn to a frazzle," "feel like two cents," and "feather one's nest."

I remember one time receiving a letter from our adopted deaf son Ronnie. He was trying to use the same expressions as his hearing friends so he wrote, "How are you? I am fit as a fiddler."

Suggestions to help you learn Sign Language more readily.

- There is no shortcut to learning the signs.
- You need to have patience.
- Do not get discouraged.
- It takes practice, practice, practice. Go over the signs again and again to get them into your mind.
- Associate with deaf people. This is the best way to get to know their language.
- Use the signs you know. Talk with your deaf friends and don't be afraid to use what you have learned.
- Learn to "think deaf." Sign Language is not learning a new way of saying the English language; it is learning a new language.
- You will find that ideas and complete thoughts are expressed. Often the verb is at the end of the sentence, as in "I town go." Prepositions and articles are generally left out. Often the deaf person will put the noun before the adjective as in "my mother house," or "my friend boy."

These four very important facts cannot be emphasized enough:
1. Learn to think deaf.
2. How fast you can sign is not as important as how well you get the message across.
3. How many signs you know is not as important as how well you use the ones you know.
4. Keep your interpreting simple, in words easily understood by a small child.

Rules for Learning Signs

1. *To learn the alphabet:*
   - Keep arms free and easy.
   - Keep palm toward the person to whom you are speaking.
   - Do not sling or slur.
   - Learn well first; add speed later.
   - Practice on these words:
     adz, fan, mop, cow, box, jar, sky, hat, quill, glove.

2. *Words with similar meanings have the same sign.* Examples include:
   - Happy, joy, glad
   - Want, longing
   - Love, dear, loving

3. *Words with different meanings have different signs.*
   - "Save," as from sin, is different from "save," as with money.
   - "Meat" is different from "meet."

4. *Tenses in Sign Language.* Deaf children today are being taught to put endings onto their signs to denote future or past tense. However, you will find the older deaf indicate future or past by signing "in the future," or "in the past."

5. *Plurals in Sign Language.* Again, today deaf children are being taught to show the "s" on the sign to denote more than one. However, the older deaf add "many, many" to the noun to show more than one. In using the word "men," "many, many" with the sign for "man" shows there are several men.

Keys to the Explanations

To help you understand how the sign is made, we will often ask you to use, on your hand, a letter in the alphabet. These will be designated as follows:

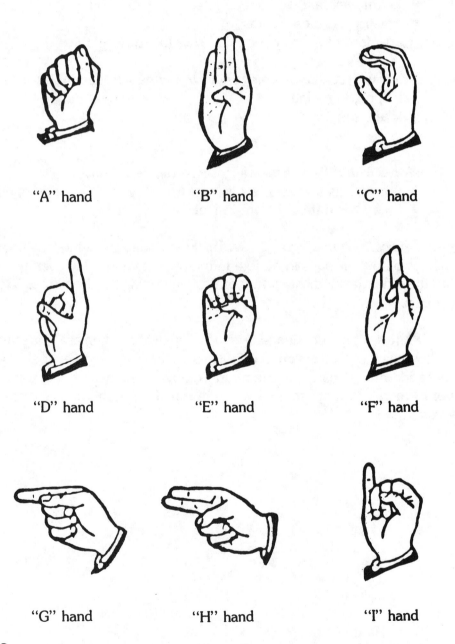

"A" hand   "B" hand   "C" hand

"D" hand   "E" hand   "F" hand

"G" hand   "H" hand   "I" hand

"J" hand

"K" hand

"L" hand

"M" hand

"N" hand

"O" hand

"P" hand

"Q" hand

"R" hand

"S" hand

"T" hand

"U" hand

"V" hand

"W" hand

"X" hand

"Y" hand

"Z" hand

There will be other positions of the hands to be used to explain how to make the signs. These will be as follows:

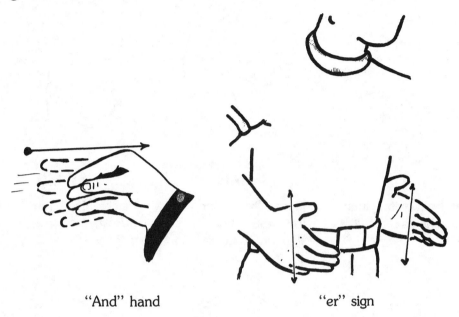

"And" hand   "er" sign

"Horizontal" hand . . . . .Hands parallel with the floor.
"Vertical" hands . . . . .Hands pointing upward.
"Inverted" hands . . . . .Hands pointing downward.
"Inward" hands . . . . .Palms toward the body.
"Outward" hands . . . . .Palms away from body.
"Palm toward palm" . . . . .Palms facing each other.
"Palm to palm" . . . . .Palms applied to each other.
"Prone" hands . . . . .Palms down.
"Supine" hands . . . . .Palms up.
"Tandem" hands . . . . .One hand behind the other in a line.
"N.S." . . . . .Indicates a "natural sign."

The middle "sensitive" finger is usually used in words of sensitivity or feeling. "Male sign" refers to signs made at the forehead and designates male gender. "Female sign" refers to signs made at the chin and designates female gender. The words in italics give a more literal interpretation for the sign and will be useful as a memory aid.

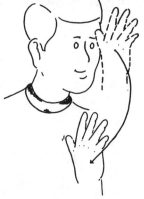

BOY

Grab hold of imaginary bill of a boy's cap. *Bill of cap.*

MAN

Bring "five" hand from forehead to chest. *Male sign on forehead and chest.*

FATHER

Place "five" hand on forehead. *Male sign on forehead.*

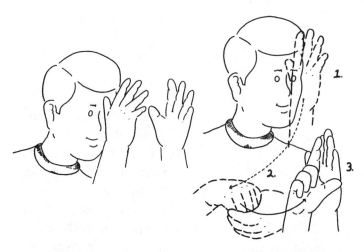

GRANDFATHER

Use two "five" hands to show two fathers. *Male signs on forehead.*

FATHER-IN-LAW

Bring "five" hand from forehead; change to "L" right hand and place on left hand. *Male sign on forehead and "L" hand for "law."*

BROTHER

Point to forehead for male sign with index finger of right hand— bring index finger down to index finger of left hand to show they are the same. *Male sign plus "same."*

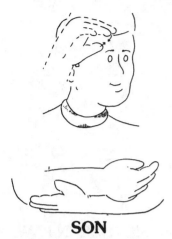

SON

Point to forehead for male sign and then cradle right arm in left arm for baby. *Male sign plus "baby."*

HUSBAND

Point to forehead for male sign; then join your hands together to show "clasp" in marriage. *Male sign plus "marriage."*

NEPHEW

Shake "N" hand at the forehead. *"N" at forehead shows male relative.*

UNCLE

Shake "U" hand at the forehead. *"U" at forehead shows male relative.*

GIRL

Draw "A" hand along lower jaw as if you are straightening a bonnet string. *Show bonnet string.*

WOMAN

Place "five" hand on chin then "five" hand on chest. *Female sign on chin.*

 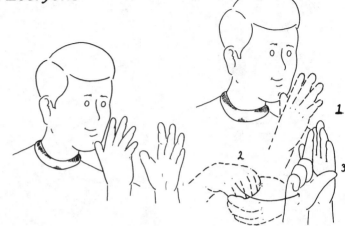

MOTHER

Place "five" hand on chin. *Female sign on chin.*

GRANDMOTHER

Use two "five" hands to show two mothers. *Female signs on chin.*

MOTHER-IN-LAW

Bring "five" hand from chin and place "L" right hand on palm of left hand. *Female sign on forehead and "L" hand for "law."*

 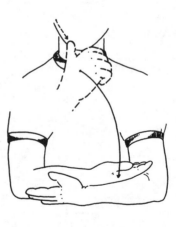 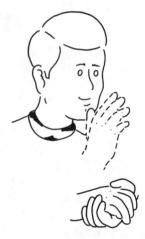

SISTER

Point to chin with index finger of right hand then bring down to index finger of left hand to show they are the same. *Female sign plus "same."*

DAUGHTER

Point to chin and then cradle right arm in left arm. *Female sign plus "baby."*

WIFE

Point to chin and then join hands together to show "clasp" in marriage. *Female sign plus "marriage."*

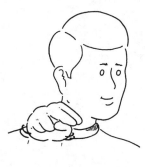

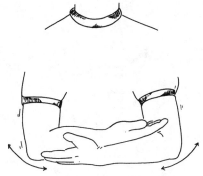

AUNT

Shake "A" hand at chin. *"A" hand at chin—female relative.*

NIECE

Shake "N" hand at side of chin. *"N" hand at chin—female relative.*

BABY

Cradle right arm in left arm as if cradling a baby. *Rocking baby.*

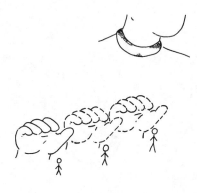

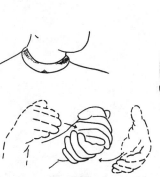

CHILDREN

Move right "prone" hand from left to right. *Show heights of several children.*

MARRY, MARRIAGE

Right hand grabs hold of left hand. *Hands clasped in marriage.*

LOVE

Press crossed arms on chest. *Pressed to one's heart.*

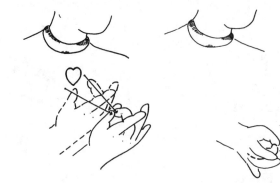

LIKE

With thumb and middle "sensitive" finger pull an imaginary string from your heart. *Pulls the heartstring.*

HATE, DESPISE

Flick middle "sensitive" finger off of thumb. *Pushing away from you.*

HOME

Place "and" hand first at mouth, then at eye. *A place to eat and sleep.*

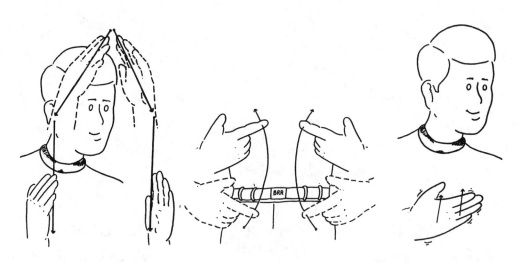

HOUSE

Make the shape of a housetop with hands. *Housetops.*

LIFE, LIVE

Make "L" sign with each hand and pass up the sides of chest. *Blood rising in body.*

HAPPY, JOY

Pat chest several times with right hand. *Bubbling inside.*

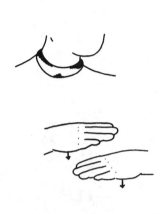

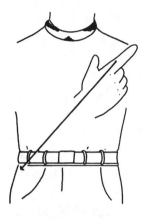

SATISFIED

Move inverted hands on chest downward. *All feeling quieted.*

LAZY

Drag "L" sign from left shoulder to right hip. *Lazy attitude of body.*

EXCITED

Use both middle "sensitive" fingers pushed upward at sides of chest several times. *Blood rushing upward.*

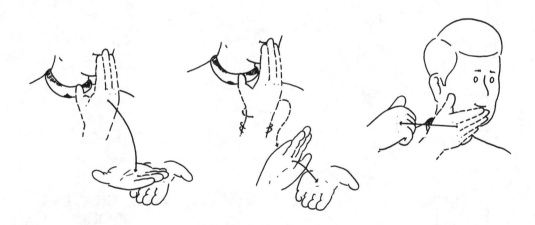

GOOD

Move vertical fingers of right hand from nose down to palm of left hand. *Smells good.*

BAD

Move vertical fingers of right hand from nose down, "palm to palm." *Smells bad.*

BETTER

Move "vertical" fingers from lips to right side of face and change to "A" hand. *More than good.*

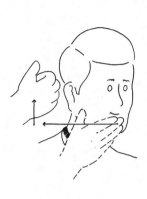

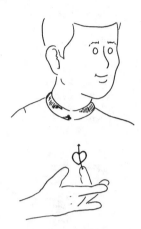

BEST

Place "vertical" hand at lips and follow by knuckles of "A" right hand hitting against knuckles of 'A" left hand. *More than good.*

THANK YOU

Move vertical fingers from lips forward to become "supine" hand. *All good.*

FEEL

Point middle "sensitive" finger to middle of chest several times. *To show sensation in midsection.*

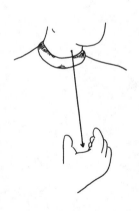

SICK

Point middle "sensitive" finger of right hand to head. Point middle "sensitive" finger of left hand to chest. *Feeling is bad in head and chest.*

HUNGRY

Draw "C" hand down chest from throat to stomach. *Gnawing pain from throat to stomach.*

WISH, CRAVING, DESIRE

Gently draw "C" hand downward at throat. *A hunger.*

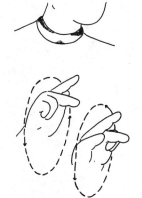

PEOPLE

Move "P" hands in circular motion toward body. *Showing several persons.*

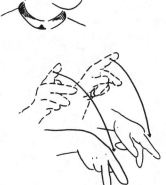

PERSON

Use "P" hand with one outward motion. *To show one.*

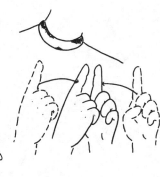

MEET, INTRODUCE

Bring "D" fingers of each hand together. *Two people being introduced.*

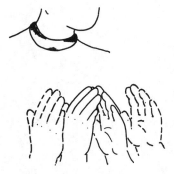

MEETING

Bring "four" hands together palm to palm. *Many people coming together.*

COUSIN

Place right vertical "C" at temple for male cousin; right vertical "C" at cheek for female cousin. *"C" for cousin.*

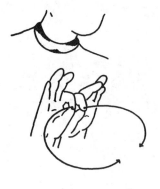

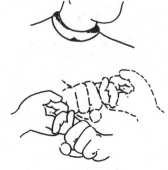

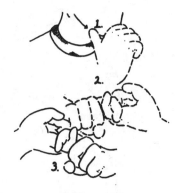

FAMILY

With "F" hands touching, make a circle to bring little fingers together. *Family circle.*

FRIEND

Hook right "X" finger on left "X" finger; then left "X" finger on right "X" finger. *Clasp in brotherly love.*

GIRL FRIEND

Make sign for girl then sign for friend.

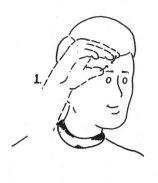

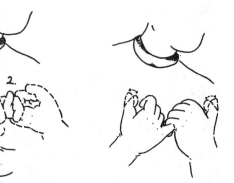

BOY FRIEND

Make sign for boy; then sign for friend.

SWEETHEART

Hook little fingers; with thumbs show two persons bowing and talking to one another. *Two persons close together.*

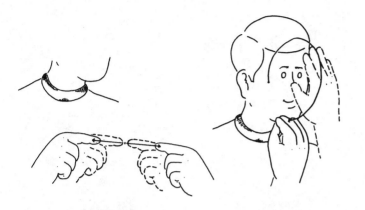

ENEMY

Draw index fingers apart to symbolize a broken friendship. *Going in opposite directions.*

PRETTY

As "five" hand circles face change to "A" hand. *Face neatly arranged.*

BEAUTIFUL

"Five" hand in front of face becomes "and" hand, then opens again to "five" hand. *All of face neatly arranged.*

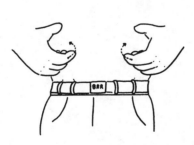

UGLY

Pull "X" finger across the nose. *Face out of shape.*

YOUNG

Use tips of fingers of both bent hands at side of chest. Brush upward briskly several times. *Blood rushing upward.*

OLD

Imitate an old man stroking his whiskers with a trembling hand.

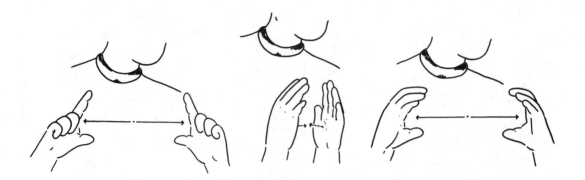

LARGE

Draw "L" hands apart. *Shows largeness.*

SMALL

With palms facing, move hands toward one another. *Shows smallness.*

GREAT

Draw cupped hands apart. *Shows greatness.*

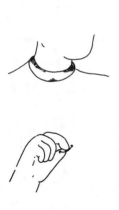

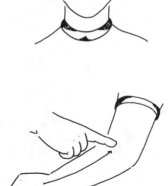

TINY, LITTLE BIT

Rub right thumb and index tip together as if something very small is between them. *Tiny as a grain of sand.*

LONG

Show measure of length on left arm with right index finger. *Shows length.*

GOD

Bring "B" hand above head down to "B" hand at chest. *God in heaven comes down to man.*

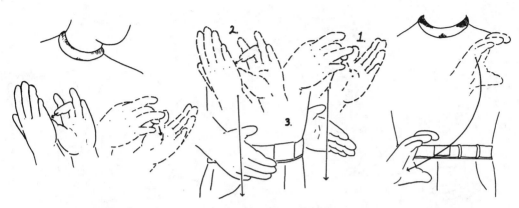

JESUS

Middle "sensitive" finger of right hand points to nail print in left palm. Middle "sensitive" finger of left hand points to nail print in right palm. *Nail prints in each hand.*

CHRISTIAN

Make sign for Jesus; then add the "er" sign. *Jesus follower.*

CHRIST

Move "C" of right hand from left shoulder to right hip. *Shows where stole of royalty is worn.*

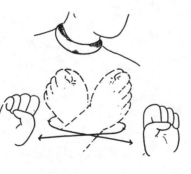

LORD

Lift "L" right hand from left shoulder to right hip. *Shows royalty.*

SAVE

Cross "S" hands to symbolize being bound by sin; then pull hands apart. *Shackles broken.*

SAVE (money)

Place "V" right hand on back of left hand to show watchful eyes on money. *Watching your money.*

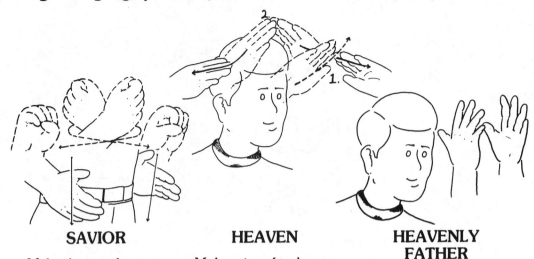

SAVIOR

Make the sign for save; then add the "er" sign.

HEAVEN

Make sign for house above head; then right hand under left to show entrance to heaven. *House in the sky.*

HEAVENLY FATHER

Make sign for heaven; then add sign for two fathers.

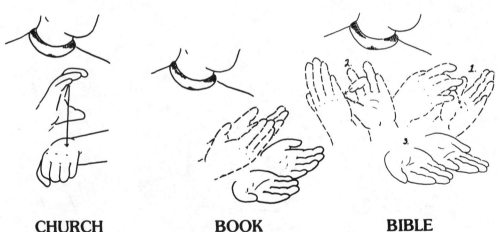

CHURCH

With left hand symbolizing a rock, bring "C" right hand to rest upon the left wrist. *Standing on the rock.*

BOOK

"Palm to palm"; then open to look like a book. *Opening a book.*

BIBLE

Make sign for Jesus; then sign for book. *Jesus Book.*

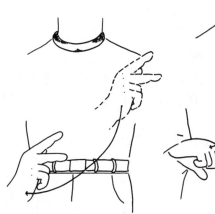

KING

Move "K" right hand from left shoulder to right hip. *Stole worn by royalty.*

QUEEN

Move "Q" right hand from left shoulder to right hip. *Stole of royalty.*

PREACH

Shake "F" hand at side of head. *A friar preaching.*

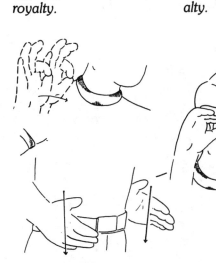

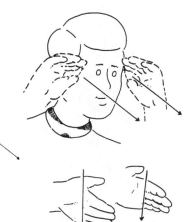

PREACHER

Make sign for preach; then "er" sign.

TEACH

Place both "and" hands at sides of forehead as if taking something out; then push hands forward. *Take from your head and put into head of others.*

TEACHER

Make sign for teach; then add "er" sign.

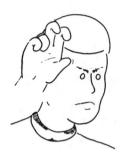

DEVIL

Place index and middle fingers of both hands at sides of head. *Shows ugly horns.*

TEMPT

Nudge elbow of left arm with index finger of right hand. *Being pushed into sin.*

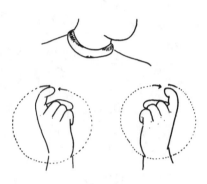

SIN

Move index fingers in a circular fashion. *Shows confusion.*

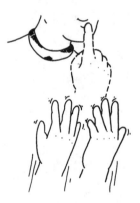

HELL

Point to lips for red; then wiggle all fingers. *Flickering of flames.*

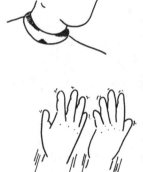

FIRE

Wiggle all fingers to show the flickering of flames. *Flickering of flames.*

PUNISH

Clench left hand as if grasping a disobedient child by the collar; strike with the right index finger. *Hold rascal with one hand; strike him with the rod.*

LESSON 1 PRACTICE

1. Children live in Uncle's house.

2. Pretty baby (is) bad.

3. Boys and girls love Jesus.

4. Jesus likes men and women.

5. Lazy people feel sick.

6. Jesus lives in heaven.

7. Good people hate sin.

8. Christ saves men, women, boys, and girls.

9. Devil tempts kings, queens, and preachers.

10. Beautiful church (is) built large.

SONGS
"Yes, Jesus Loves Me."
"The B-I-B-L-E"

MEMORY VERSE
"God is love."—1 John 4:8

LESSON 2

NOT

Move thumb tip of "A" hand out from under and away from chin.

TRUE

Move right vertical index finger straight out from lips. *Straight talk.*

BE

Use "B" hand.

IS

Use "I" hand.

WAS

Use "W" hand and then "S" hand.

ARE

Use "R" hand.

AM

Use "A" hand.

WERE

Use "W" hand and then "R" hand.

BEEN

Use "B" hand and then "N" hand.

 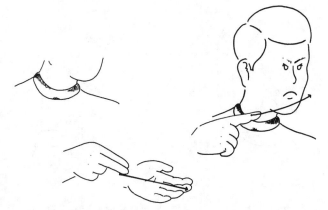

BEING

Use "B" hand and then "ing" suffix.

HONEST

Draw "H" right hand down left hand from wrist to the tip of middle finger. *Straight dividing.*

LIE, FALSE

Push right index finger, palm downward, across the lips from right to left. *Crooked talk.*

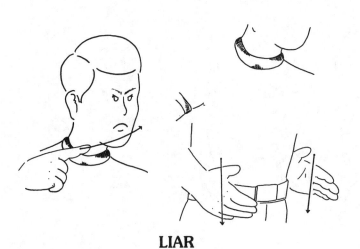

LIAR

Make sign for lie; then the "er" sign.

MISTAKE

Place "Y" hand on chin. *Spoke out of turn.*

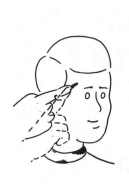

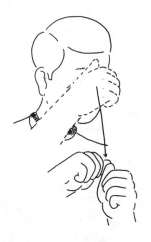

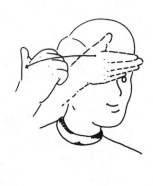

THINK

Bore tip of right index finger into forehead. *Boring into brain.*

REMEMBER

Bring tip of right thumb, from forehead down to nail on thumb of left hand. *Thoughts stay.*

FORGET

Move horizontal "B" hand from in front of forehead to the right and change to "A" hand. *Thought washed out of mind.*

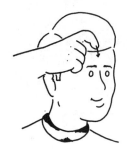

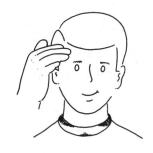

UNDERSTAND

Flick index finger off thumb in front of forehead. *Thought is opened up.*

WISE, WISDOM

Strike downward "X" finger at forehead several times. *All is in the head.*

KNOW

Place tip of right "B" hand, palm inward, against the forehead. *It's in your head.*

SMART

Flick middle "sensitive" finger off forehead quickly while turning hand away from face. *Sharp as a razor.*

DUMB

Thump "A" hand against the forehead several times. *Hardheaded.*

STUPID, IGNORANT

Place the back of "K" hand against the forehead. *Knowledge cannot penetrate the skull.*

41

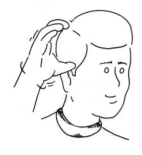 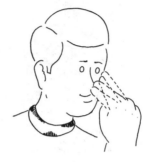 

CRAZY

Twist "C" hand at side of the head. *Brains mixed up.*

FUNNY

Move "H" hand down nose several times. *Wrinkling of the nose as in smiling.*

SILLY

Twist "Y" hand in front of face several times. *Revolving brain on wheels.*

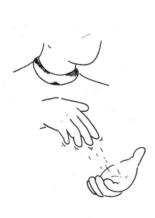 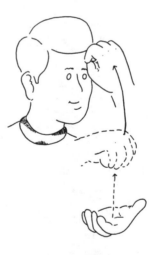 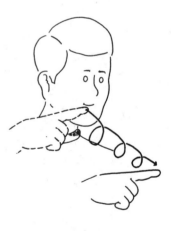

STUDY

Oscillating fingers of right hand, move from prone left hand upward to forehead. *Knowledge going from page to brain.*

LEARN

"And" right hand from "prone" left hand to forehead. *Take from book and put into head.*

TELL, SPEAK

Bring index finger of right hand from lips and rotate away from mouth. *Words roll out of mouth.*

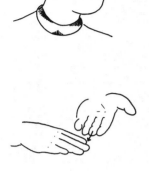

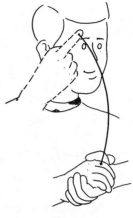

EXCUSE, FORGIVE

Rub fingertips of right "B" hand on heel of left prone hand several times. *Rub out mistake.*

BLOOD

Draw "five" hand with fingers wiggling from lips and over back of left hand. *Hemorrhage.*

BELIEVE

Point to head with right index finger and then join hands as if taking hold of something. *Knowledge in your head that you grab hold of.*

DON'T BELIEVE

Draw right "V" hand away from eyes. *Pull off the blindfold.*

DON'T CARE

Place "and" hand in front of eyes; turn hand outward to become "five" hand. *Throw the thought out of mind.*

BLESS

Place both "A" hands at each side of mouth; turn them outward to "supine" hands in front of body. *Shows hands on heads of children.*

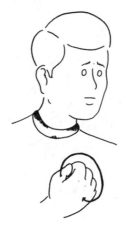

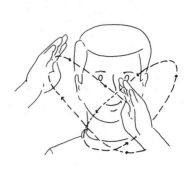

PLEASE

"Move "five" hand in a circular fashion on chest. *Pleasant internal feeling.*

SORRY

"A" hand revolving on chest. *Grinding of heart.*

TROUBLE

Move both "five" hands alternately in a circular motion in front of body. *Everything wrong coming at me.*

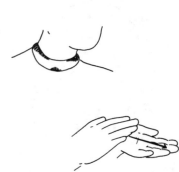

SWEET

Flick "W" hand off chin. *Drips off chin like honey.*

CUTE

Flick "H" hand off chin. *Shows sweetness.*

NICE, CLEAN

Brush left palm with right palm from wrist to tips of fingers. *Brushing every speck of dirt away.*

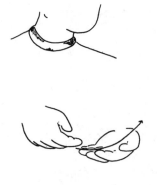

NEW

Dip fingertips of right hand into palm of left hand. *New metal pushed out of mold.*

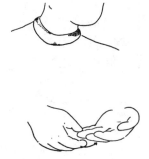

EASY

Lift fingertips of left hand with fingertips of right hand. *Fingers easily lifted.*

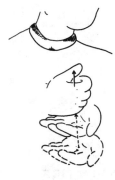

HELP

Lift right "A" hand with left "prone" hand. *Giving a lift.*

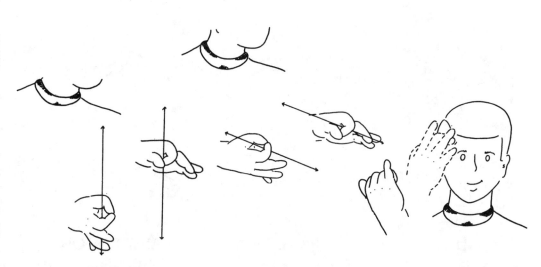

JUDGE

Move "F" hands up and down alternately. *The balancing of the scales.*

EXPLAIN

Move "F" hands in and out from the body alternately. *Untangling the tangles.*

WHY

Flick middle "sensitive" finger off forehead. *Wondering from the seat of reason.*

  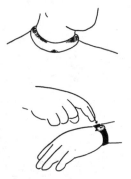

BECAUSE

Vertical hand at forehead becomes "A" hand in front of face. *Explanation from seat of reason.*

FOR

Touch index finger to forehead then push away from forehead, turning outward. *Thoughts put forward.*

TIME

Index finger of right hand points to wrist of left hand. *Wrist watch.*

  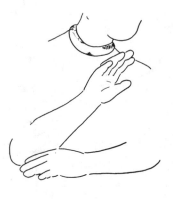

DAY

Move "D" hand from right side of body in a circular fashion over to left side of body. *Sun rising in the east, setting in the west.*

MORNING

Left arm against body represents horizon; bring right "supine" hand up under the left arm. *Sun rising.*

AFTERNOON

Left arm against body represents horizon; move right "prone" hand forward over left arm. *Sun setting.*

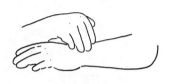
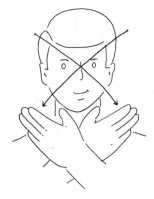

NIGHT

Left arm against body represents horizon; push right "prone" hand far over left arm as the sun sinks. *Sun below horizon.*

DARK

Pass vertical hands, palms inward, across the face until hands are crossed at wrists. *Shades pulled over eyes.*

YESTERDAY

Move "Y" hand backward from mouth to ear. *In the past.*

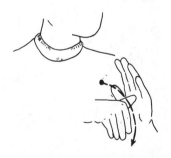
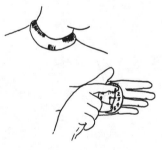

TOMORROW

Move thumb of right "A" hand from lower jaw forward. *In the future.*

AFTERWHILE

Using left palm as the face of the clock, put fingertips of "D" right hand against left palm and turn the "D" hand. *Shows clock hand moving.*

MINUTE, SECOND

Using left palm as the face of the clock, put fingertips of "D" right hand against left palm and move slightly. *Time barely moves.*

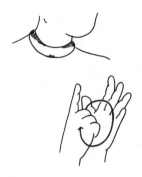

HOUR

Using left palm as the face of the clock, put fingertips of "D" right hand against left palm; make a full turn. *Hand of clock has made a full circle.*

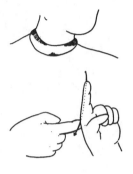

MONTH

Joints of left "D" finger represent the four weeks of a month. Right "D" finger moves from top joint of left finger to lowest joint. *Weeks passing.*

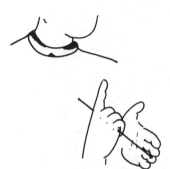

WEEK

Left "supine" palm represents the calendar. Right "D" hand passes from heel to tips of fingers of left hand to show one row of dates is gone. *One week of month gone.*

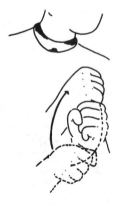

YEAR

Place right "S" hand on left "S" hand. Lift right "S" and move it around the left "S" hand. *Earth making a complete circle around the sun.*

PAST, BEFORE

Move right vertical hand over right shoulder. *Back into the past.*

BEFORE (as going before or standing before)

Hold both vertical hands in front of body, palm to palm; move them outward. *Standing before a person or thing.*

Instructions for Converting Individual Words into Signs

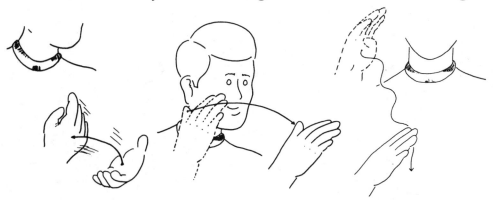

BEFORE TIME

Move right vertical hand over right shoulder. *Back into the past.*

FUTURE

Move open right hand, with palm leftward, foward. *Forward into future.*

NEVER

Move open right hand, with palm leftward, back and forth in a waving motion. *Head shaking "no".*

FIRST

Index finger of right hand points to thumb of left hand.

LAST

Little finger of right hand points to little finger of left hand.

NEAR

Place left palm near body with fingers pointing to the right; bring palm of right hand to back of left hand. *One hand near other hand.*

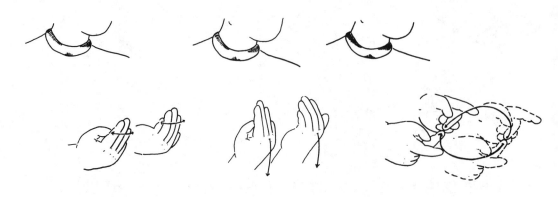

HERE

Place both "supine" palms, with fingers pointing outward, in front of body. *Right before you.*

NOW

Cup both "supine" hands in front of body; drop them slightly. *Right here in front of us.*

PLACE

Make a circle with both "P" hands in front of body to show limits of place. *Limits drawn off.*

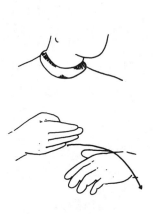

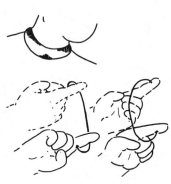

AFTER

Hold left arm horizontally and push edge of right hand over back of left hand. *Just behind.*

LATE

Right hand held at side of body with fingers pointing down moves backwards several times. *You are behind time.*

WHEN

Move index fingers of both hands in a circular motion toward each other. *What hour on the clock?*

Instructions for Converting Individual Words into Signs

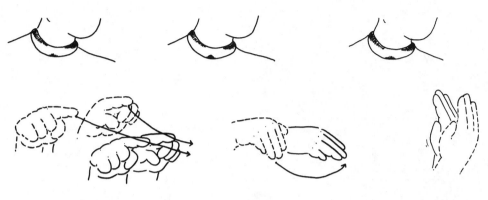

DURING, WHILE, AS

Hold both index fingers near body; then move them downward and forward. *Going into future.*

GO

Move one or both hands away from body. *Motioning someone to go.*

COME

Move one or both hands toward body. *Beckoning someone to come.*

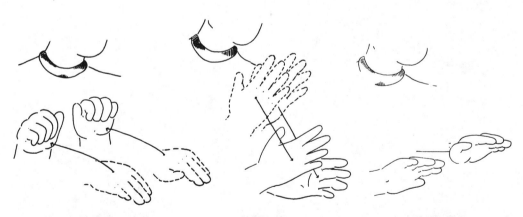

LEAVE, DEPART

Extend "prone" hands side by side; draw them toward body and form "A" hands. *A person trying to make room for others to pass.*

LEAVE

Move both hands, palm to palm, forward and downward. *Placing object on table.*

WALK

Prone hands pointing outward, move down alternately as if walking with them. *Imitating feet walking.*

RUN

Hook right index finger onto thumb of left hand; move forward. *Skipping along.*

PLAY

Shake horizontal "Y" hand up and down in front of body several times. *Action shown.*

FAST, QUICK

Flick right thumb off index finger as if shooting a marble. *Quick as a flash.*

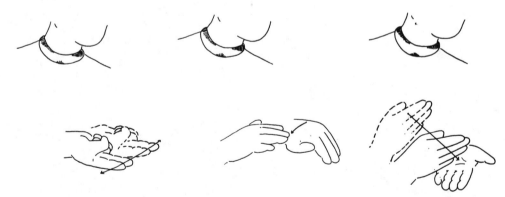

HURRY

Move "H" hand in a circular fashion. *Show motion.*

SLOW

Extend left arm outward and draw right hand slowly up left arm from wrist toward shoulder. *Dragging along.*

STOP

Hit palm of left hand with edge of right hand. *There is a barrier.*

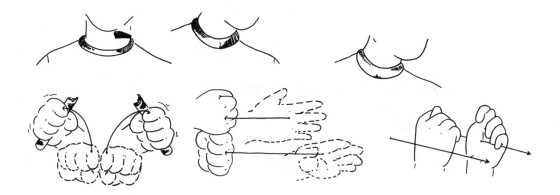

BREAK

Using both "S" hands, act as if breaking a stick in two. *Breaking in two.*

GET

Change "five" hands to "S" hands; place right "S" on top of left "S" *Gathering and holding.*

TRY

Push both "T" hands away from body. *Pushing.*

LESSON 2 PRACTICE

1. Teach children (to) love God.

2. God bless truth, wisdom, and understanding.

3. Study and learn (to) tell others.

4. Weeks, months, and years go fast.

5. Yesterday morning I ran slow.

6. Stop, try (to) get help (for the) judge.

7. Nice, new place (is) near home.

8. Funny, silly boys forget (to) study.

9. Tomorrow night come play.

10. The judge forgave and explained why (it is) easy (to) sin.

SONGS
"I Love Him"
"I Have the Joy, Joy, Joy"

MEMORY VERSE
"We love Him [use sign for God] because He
first loved us."—1 John 4:19.
29

LESSON 3

STAND

Stand right inverted "V" fingers on left "supine" palm. *Standing legs.*

SIT

Place right prone "H" hand on left prone "H" hand with right fingers hanging down. *Legs over edge of seat.*

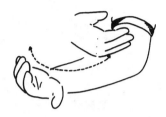

SING, SONG

Extend left arm; move right hand to and fro over left arm from wrist to shoulder. *Imitating a song leader.*

SMELL

Move right "supine" palm up and down several times in front of nose. *Smelling perfume on palm of hand.*

EAT, FOOD

Place right "and" fingertips repeatedly at the lips. *Putting food to the mouth.*

TASTE

Place middle "sensitive" finger of open hand just below bottom lip. *Placing on tongue to taste.*

DRY

Draw right "X" finger across lips from left to right. *Lips are dry.*

THIRSTY

Draw right "X" finger across lips from left to right; bring "D" finger down throat from chin to collar bone. *Throat is dry.*

WATER

Place right vertical "W" just below bottom lip. *Show drinking water.*

HEAR

Point right index finger to ear. *Point to organ of hearing.*

DEAF

Point right index finger to lips and then to ear. *Can't speak or hear.*

BLIND

Place fingertips of right "V" hand just below each eye. *Sight is closed.*

SEE

Place fingertips of right "V" hand just beneath each *eye*; then move hand outward. *Eyes can see.*

LOOK, WATCH

Place fingertips of right "V" hand just beneath each *eye*; turn hand outward. *Eyes are looking.*

BLUSH

Point right index finger at lips (meaning red) and then place fingertips of "and" hand on cheek and open hand. *Red spreads over face.*

ASHAMED, EMBARRASSED

Place backs of both hands, fingers pointing downward, against the cheeks; move hands upward. *Hiding the face.*

WARM

Move "five" hand from right side of face across mouth, changing to "S" hand. *Too hot for mouth.*

HOT (as in weather)

Draw right index finger across forehead from left to right. *Flicking perspiration off the forehead.*

57

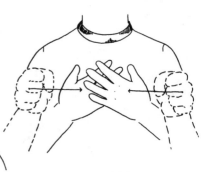

HOT (as in food)

Place "and" hand at mouth as if taking something out; turn hand suddenly to palm outward as if to drop the hot article. *Too hot for mouth.*

COLD

Shake both "S" hands in front of body. *Shivering from cold.*

AFRAID, SCARED

Place "S" hands in front of body; open them into "five" hands as they move toward one another. Make this sign with more force to convey "scared." *Shows fear.*

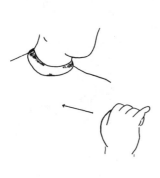

I

"I" hand in front of body is brought to chest; rest thumb on chest.

ME

Point to self with right index finger.

MY, MINE

Place right palm on chest. *Belonging to me.*

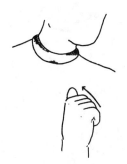

MYSELF

Place "A" hand on chest. *It is mine.*

HIMSELF, HERSELF

With "A" hand, point to the person in reference. *Something belongs to him or to her.*

YOURSELVES

Draw "A" hand from right to left indicating several persons. *Something belonging to several.*

YOU

Point right index finger at the person you are talking with.

THEY

Point right index finger at several things or persons in the distance.

ANY

Shake right "A" hand with thumb upward while moving it from left to right in front of the body. *Waving motion shows any individual or thing.*

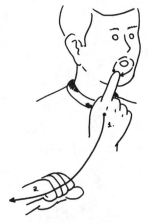

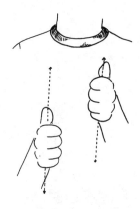

WHO

With right index finger, make a circle around pursed lips. *Point to lips formed to say "who."*

WHOEVER

Make the sign for "who"; then the sign for "any."

WHICH, OR

Move both "A" hands, thumbs upward, up and down alternately. *Offering first one and then the other.*

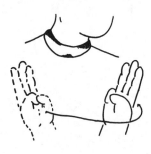

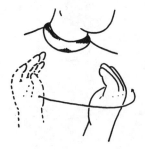

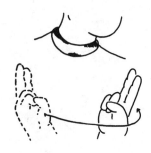

WE

Move "W" hand from right shoulder outward and around to left shoulder. *Point to self, then to others, and back to self.*

OUR

Move right vertical palm from right shoulder outward and around to left shoulder. *Yours and mine.*

US

Move right "U" finger from right shoulder outward and around to left shoulder. *Pointing to myself and to you.*

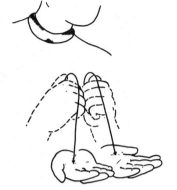

HOW

Roll middle knuckles of fingers of both hands together from index fingers to little fingers, then open to supine hands. *Opened up and out.*

ALL

Starting with fingertips of right supine hand in left palm, make a circle with right "five" hand bringing it back to rest in left palm. *Embracing all things.*

ALL RIGHT

Push edge of right hand across left supine palm. *Proceed onward.*

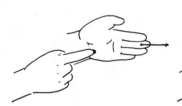

SHOW YOU

Place tip of right index finger on the heel of left palm; move both hands forward. *Showing someone something in palm.*

SHOW ME

Place tip of right index finger on heel of left palm; move both hands toward body.

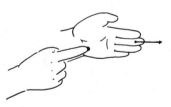

SHOW OFF

Place tip of right index finger on heel of left palm; push both hands forward rapidly several times.

61

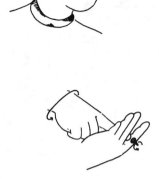

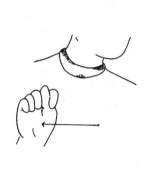

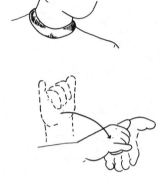

BEGIN

Twist tip of right index finger in between left index and middle fingers. *Starting to drive a screw.*

THE

Move "T" hand from left to right in front of body.

THAT

Drop right "Y" hand into palm of left hand.

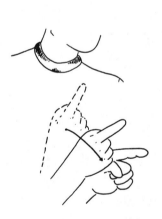

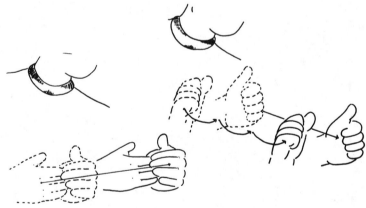

RIGHT, CORRECT

Strike right "G" hand against left "G" hand. *It is good.*

LEAD

Grasp left fingertips with fingers and thumb of right hand and draw hand to right. *Right hand leads left hand.*

FOLLOW

Move right "A" hand behind left "A" hand. *One hand follows the other.*

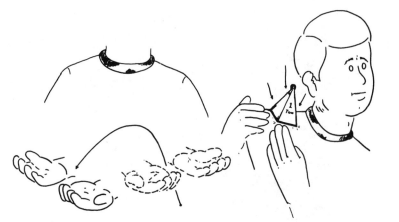

CARRY

Move both supine hands from left to right. *Carry something from one place to another.*

BURDEN, RESPONSIBILITY

Bear down with tips of prone right and left hands on right shoulder. *It rests on my shoulders.*

BLAME, FAULT

Rest right "A" hand on prone left hand. *Carrying the burden.*

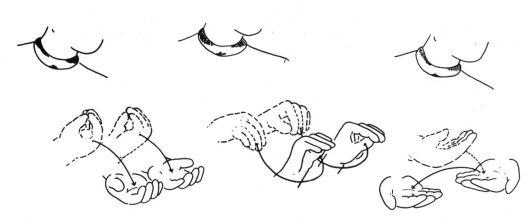

GIVE, PRESENT, GIFT

Change "and" hands to supine hands while moving hands away from self. *Open hands to give.*

SELL

Position both "and" hands, fingers pointing downward in front of body. *Holding a garment for inspection.*

BUY

Right "and" hand moves outward from left supine hand. *Giving money to clerk.*

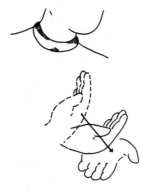

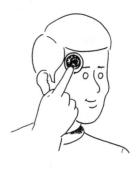

MONEY

Place back of right hand in left supine palm; repeat several times. *Placing money in palm of hand.*

DOLLARS

Draw right index finger and thumb from heel to fingertips of left palm. *Edges of dollar bills traced on palm of hand.*

CENTS

Make a circle on right side of forehead with right index finger. *Circle for penny on forehead near dark hair.*

CHANGE (money)

Edge of right hand moves back and forth on left edgewise hand from tip of index finger to thumb. *Hand changing places.*

CHANGE

Place both "X" hands together at first knuckle of middle fingers; twist hands back and forth. *Break into pieces.*

EMPTY

Hold left "O" hand like a cup; draw right "and" hand down through left hand. *Gone down and out the bottom.*

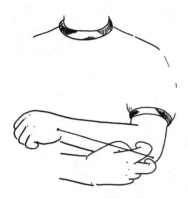

STEAL

Bend left arm toward right shoulder; draw bent fingers of right "V" hand from from elbow to wrist. *Taking something from under a person's arm.*

WILL

Move right "five" hand from side of face forward. *Into future.*

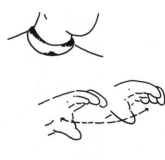

DO, ACT, ACTING

With both "C" hands prone in front of body, move them first to one side and then to the other. *Action as in polishing or scrubbing.*

CAN

Bring both "S" horizontal hands down with force. *Fists brought down showing power.*

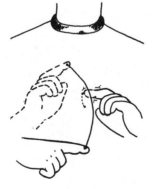

CAN'T

With prone hands, strike left index finger with right index finger. *Can't knock down to stay.*

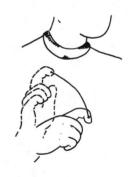

MUST

Bring right "X" finger down with force. *Shows determination.*

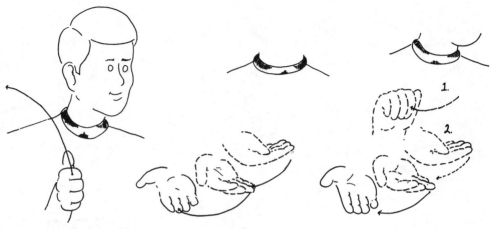

WON'T, REFUSE

Throw right "S" hand forcefully over right shoulder. *Refuse to accept.*

THING

Move right "five" supine hand from left to right. *Placing several things on the table top.*

ANYTHING

Make sign for "any"; then sign for "thing."

EVERY, EACH

Rub knuckles of right "A" hand several times on thumb of left "A" hand. *Right thumb pointing to individuals.*

EVERY (Daily)

Draw thumb of right "A" hand along lower jaw.

EVERYTHING

Make sign for "every"; then sign for "thing."

66

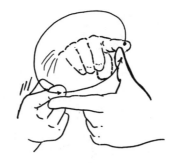

THEN

Point index finger of right hand at thumb of left hand, then at index finger of left hand. *First one, then the other.*

AND THEN

Draw index finger of right hand from tip of index finger of left hand down the length of the finger and up the thumb.

AND

As right "four" hand moves from left to right, it changes to "and" hands. *Two sentences joined together.*

THAN

Hit fingertips of right prone hand against fingertips of left prone hand. *Pushing down to show lowered degree.*

ON

Place prone fingers of right hand on back of left prone hand. *Placing on top.*

AT

Place right fingertips against edge of left prone hand. *You are right "at" it.*

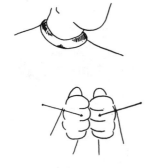 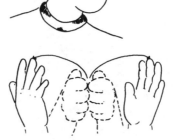 

WITH, TOGETHER	**WITHOUT**	**UNDER**

Bring both "A" hands together, thumbs upward. *Both hands together.*

Make sign for "with," then open fingers to point outward.

Place right "A" hand, thumb upward, under left prone hand. *One hand under other.*

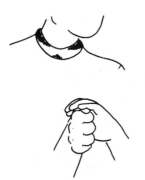 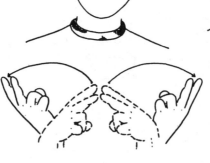 

HIDE	**VERY**	**FROM**

With right thumb of "A" hand pointing upward, close left palm down over it. *Hiding right thumb.*

Touch fingertips of "V" hands; pull apart to each side of body. *To show extent or degree.*

Pull right index finger away from left index finger and make "X" finger.

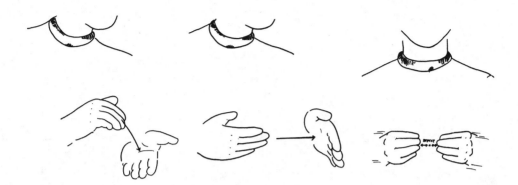

AGAIN

Fingertips of right hand hit repeatedly on palm of left vertical hand. *Place it there once more.*

AGAINST

Make sign for "again" more rapidly.

MORE

Both "and" hands touching tips of fingers repeatedly. *Adding a little at a time.*

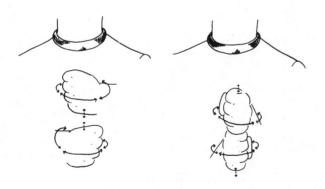

MAKE

Twist and turn right "S" hand on top of left "S" hand. *Action of twisting and pounding.*

FINISHED
(the end)

Move edge of right hand down left arm and hand to end of fingers, then drop right hand straight down. *Loose ends cut off.*

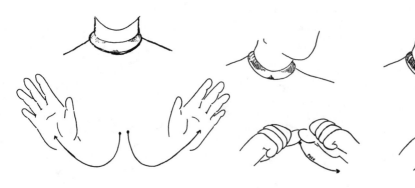

FINISHED
(completed)

Place both "five" hands, fingers downward, in front of body; bring both hands forward and upward. *It's all over.*

STAY

Thumb of right "A" hand holds down thumb of left "A" hand.

CONTINUE

Make sign for "stay" then push forward. *Keeps staying.*

LESSON 3 PRACTICE

1. We (are) dry; give us water.

2. I blame you for stealing my money.

3. Sing again (and) again with my father.

4. Everyone (person) stays (to) eat with the deaf.

5. Stand (to) sing and sit (to) hear the preacher.

6. Begin leading all (the) people (to) do right.

7. Make more nice, clean and better books.

8. Who (is) ashamed (to) help the blind man.

9. Look and see which (is) all right.

10. We will sell our home.

SONGS
"I'll Be True"
"Jesus, Jesus, Jesus, Sweetest Name"

MEMORY VERSE

"Jesus said, I [use sign for Jesus] am the way,
the truth and the life: no man cometh
to God but through [Jesus]."—John 14:6.

LESSON 4

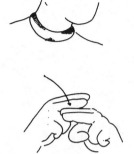

NAME

Make an "X" with right "H" hand on left "H" hand. *Making the mark of those who cannot write their names.*

POOR

Bend left arm toward right shoulder; right fingers and thumb pull at elbow of left arm. *Hole in sleeve at elbow.*

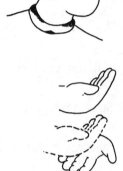

RICH

Right supine hand brought up above palm of left hand. *Money piled high.*

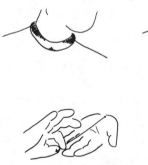

COUNT

Move fingertips of right "F" hand from heel of left hand to tips of fingers. *Counting from list in hand.*

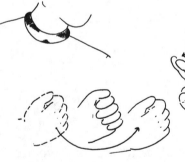

PASS

Right "A" hand passes left "A" hand. *One passes the other.*

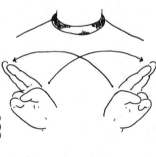

READY

Place both "R" hands together, then pull apart.

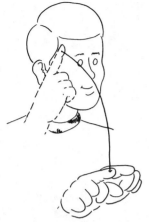

AGREE

Make sign for "think," then sign for "same."

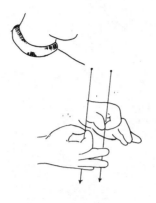

DECIDE

Place right index finger against forehead, then bring both "F" hands down in front of body. *Thoughts weighed.*

ANSWER

Place tip of right index finger at lips; then point index fingers outward. *Speak you.*

FULL

Left "O" hand represents cup; brush right prone hand over left "O" toward body. *Level with the top.*

ENOUGH

Make sign for "full." Brush over top of left "O" hand with right prone hand first toward body, then away from body. *Filled and running over.*

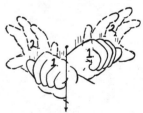

HABIT

Bring right "A" hand down on left "A" hand at wrist. *Bound by it.*

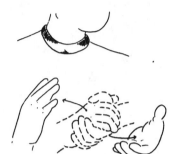

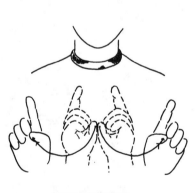

BECAME, BECOME

Place hands, palm to palm, fingers pointing outward; right hand makes a complete turn with fingers toward body. *Complete reversal of hands shows change.*

ENGAGE

Right "E" hand makes a circle over left ring finger.

SEPARATE

Clasp hands; move right hand rightward and left hand leftward. *To move apart.*

DIVORCE

Bring fingers of "D" hands together, then pull apart. *Bond is broken.*

FALL

Place right inverted "V" in left supine palm; "V" falls off to one side. *Standing legs fall to one side.*

ARISE

Place right "V" fingers in left supine palm; bring right "V" to stand on tips of fingers on left palm. *Lying down, now standing.*

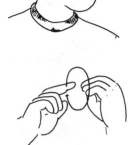

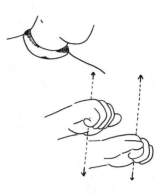

AROUND

Right index finger makes a complete circle around left "and" fingers. *Going around.*

OFTEN

Tips of fingers on right hand hit repeatedly on horizontal palm of left hand. *Again and again.*

DOUBT

Move "A" hands up and down alternately. *Thoughts weighed.*

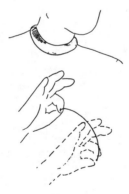

SEEK, SEARCH, CURIOUS

Right "C" hand passed across forehead from right to left in a circular motion. *Looking for something with a magnifying glass.*

FIND

Right index finger and thumb reach down and pick up an imaginary object.

MANY

Open "O" hands repeatedly in front of body. *Counting by tens.*

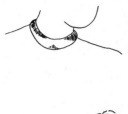

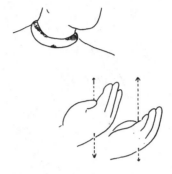

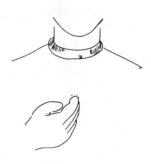

WASTE

Right "O" hand in left palm becomes "five" hand as it is lifted and turned away from body. *Throw it away.*

MAYBE, PERHAPS

Move supine hands, fingers pointing outward, up and down alternately. *Balancing of open hands shows doubt or wavering.*

HAVE

Tips of fingers of right hand hit against chest. *My or mine.*

BOTH

Bring right "V" fingers down through left "C" hand that closes as right "V" passes through. *Two together.*

SAME

Place index fingers side by side; move from right to left. *Both fingers look alike and move alike.*

DIFFERENT

Place index fingers side by side; move in different directions. *Opposite.*

OTHER

Turn right prone "A" hand over and move it to right. *Pointing to another.*

NO

Rest right index and middle finger on tip of thumb. *"N" and "O" contracted to a single motion.*

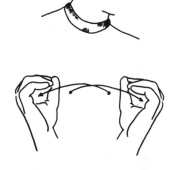

NONE, NOTHING

Place both "O" hands together; move right hand rightward and left hand leftward. *Zero amount.*

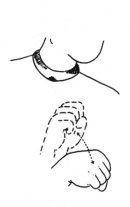

YES

Shake right "Y" hand up and down. *Head nodding affirmatively.*

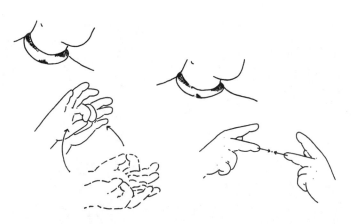

IMPORTANT, WORTH

Place tips of "F" fingers together; make a complete circle; then bring hands together again. *Raised to show superlative degree.*

PERFECT

Both "P" hands make a circle and come together, middle fingers touching.

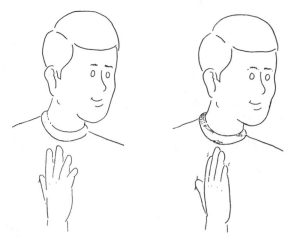

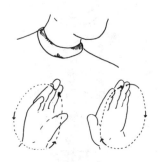

FINE, POLITE

Touch thumb of right hand, palm leftward, beneath right shoulder. *Fancy ruffles formerly worn by gentlemen.*

WONDERFUL, ADMIRE

Push vertical hands palms outward, forward several times. *Hands held up in admiration.*

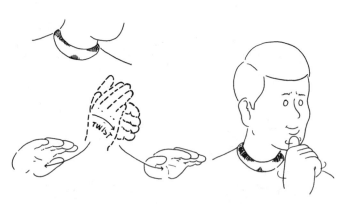

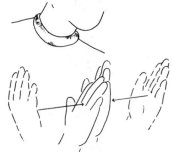

PEACE

Right hand grasps back of left hand; then left hand grasps back of right hand. *All shake hands.*

PATIENCE

Press tip of thumb of right "A" hand just beneath the bottom lip. *Lips will not complain.*

PRAISE

Clap hands several times. *Applause given.*

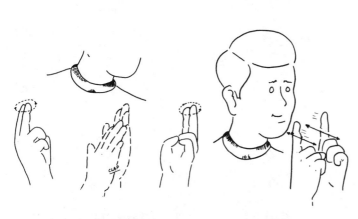

HALLELUJAH

Make sign for "praise" then raise both "H" hands in circular motion.

TALK

Touch "D" hands at knuckles; move hands back and forth. *Two people talking.*

SPEAK

Move right "five" hand forward from right side of mouth several times.

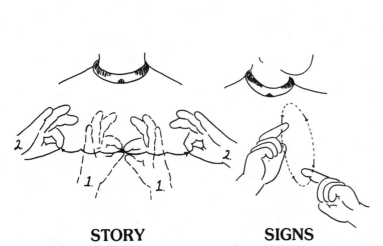

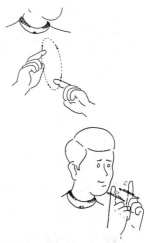

STORY

Touch tips of both "F" fingers, then move apart in a spiral motion. *Tale unravelled.*

SIGNS

With "D" hands, make circular motion toward body, alternately. *Moving the hands as if making signs.*

SIGN TALK

Make sign for "signs" and then sign for "talk."

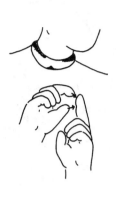

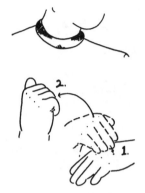

WORD

With thumb and index fingertip of right hand, measure first joint of left index finger. *One separate part of a sentence.*

CALL

Right fingertips tap back of left prone hand several times. *Tapping hand for attention.*

IMPROVING

Move right hand, edgewise, up left arm from wrist to elbow. *Stages of improvement.*

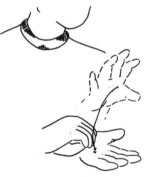

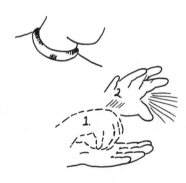

NOT IMPROVING

Move right hand edgewise down left arm from elbow to wrist. *Stages of degeneration.*

COPY

Change right "five" hand to "and" hand as right hand is placed in left palm. *Take from one page to put on another page.*

EXAMPLE

Right "and" hand in left palm becomes "five" hand as it is lifted from left palm. *Let your light shine.*

PRACTICE

Rub knuckles of right "A" hand against left index finger several times. *Polishing to make perfect.*

TEASE

Strike right "X" hand with force against thumb of left "X" hand. *One hand hitting the other savagely.*

CRUEL

Make sign for "tease" with greater force. *Tormenting, persecuting.*

WORK

Strike right "S" hand against back of wrist of left "S" hand several times. *Hammering to show effort.*

HARD WORK

Forcefully strike right bent "H" fingers against back of wrist of left bent "H" fingers.

SCHOOL

Clap heel of left supine hand with right prone hand. *Teacher claps hands for attention.*

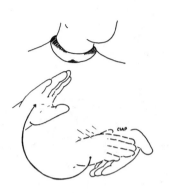

COLLEGE

Place right prone hand crosswise on left supine hand; lift right hand and move it in a clockwise fashion to make a circle; then replace it in palm of left hand. *Higher education.*

HIGH SCHOOL

Raise both "C" hands in front of body slightly; slap heel of left supine hand with heel of right prone hand. *Higher education.*

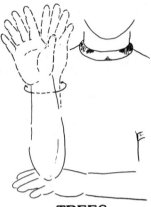

TREES

With right arm in vertical position, shake hand back and forth. *Leaves blowing in the breeze.*

FLOWERS

Pass right "and" hand from right cheek to left cheek near nose. *Smells good.*

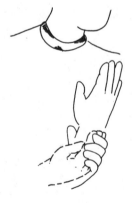

GROWING

Push right "and" fingers up through left "O." As the right hand comes through the left, right "and" opens up to a "five" hand. *Breaking through the ground.*

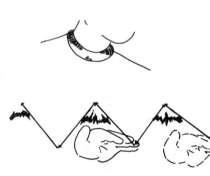

MOUNTAINS

Move both prone hands from right side of body upward to form mountain peak and downward to left side. *Mountain tops shown.*

RIVERS

Place right "W" at mouth; then move prone hands forward in a rippling fashion. *Rippling of water.*

LIGHT, BRIGHT, CLEAR

Place "and" hands at corner of each eye; change to "five" hands and move forward. *Brilliance of light shining forth.*

SUN

With right index finger trace the sun's outline at right side of head; then change to "and" hand which opens up to "five" hand as hand descends downward. *Sun spreading rays downward.*

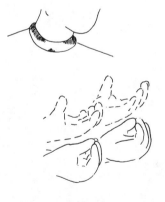

MOON

Place right vertical "C" hand at corner of right eye. *The crescent seen in the sky.*

SOFT

Open and close both "and" hands, fingers pointing upward. *Squeezing a soft ball.*

RAIN

Lower prone hands while fingers oscillate. *Raindrops falling.*

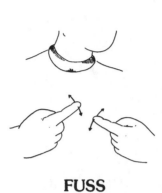

SNOW

Rest prone hands on the shoulders; then turn hands outward as fingers oscillate. *Snowflakes on shoulders.*

FUSS

Move "D" hands up and down alternately. *Two debating.*

FIGHT

Use both "S" fists to strike out alternately. *Pounding one another.*

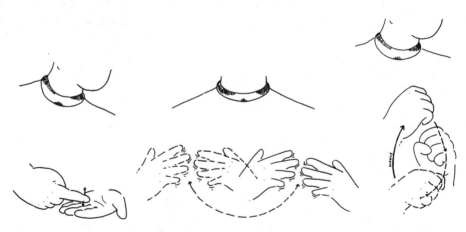

ARGUE

Strike right index finger on left supine palm several times. *Tapping the palm in an argument.*

WAR, BATTLE

Point fingers of both hands toward one another; palms inward, move rightward, then leftward. *Fingers represent soldiers on each side, advancing and retreating as they wage war.*

SUFFER

Both "S" hands circle around each other slowly with tension. *Tense fists indicate severe suffering.*

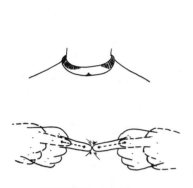

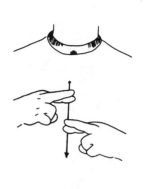

HURT, PAIN

Jab index fingers of "D" hands toward each other repeatedly. *Nerves are pierced with needles.*

TIRED

Rest tips of open hands against body; allow hands to drop as tips remain stationary against body. *Hands fall into lap with weariness.*

REST

Cross arms in front of body, hands prone; allow both arms to drop. *Arms folded in rest.*

MEAN, WORST

Place "A" hands palm to palm; strike right "A" hand downward against knuckles of left "A" hand. *Trying to beat the other person down.*

ELECTRIC

Strike right "X" finger against the left "X" finger several times. *Feeling the tinge of an electric shock.*

STUCK-UP

Push nose up with right index finger. *Nose in the air.*

  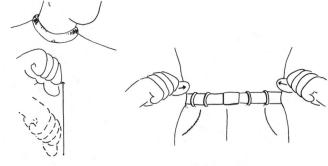

BORED

Bore right index finger into side of nose. *It digs in.*

PROUD

Draw tip of thumb of right "A" hand up the chest. *Chest swells with pride.*

BOAST

Both "A" hands hit repeatedly on each hip. *Hands on hip in an arrogant manner.*

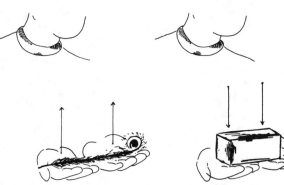  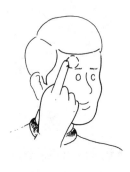

LIGHT (weight)

Lift supine hands, fingers pointed outward, with little effort. *Light as a feather.*

HEAVY

Lift supine hands, fingers pointing outward, with real effort. *Heavy as a rock.*

WONDER

Right index finger makes a circle on the right side of forehead. *Thoughts going around and around in your mind.*

LESSON 4 PRACTICE

1. What (is) your name?

2. My name (is) _____

   My sign name _____

3. The habit became hard to break.

4. Run and pass (the) poor man and help him.

5. We agreed and decided to separate.

6. Have patience and wonderful peace will come.

7. Many people waste time that (is) important.

8. Sing "praise" and "hallelujah" to our heavenly Father.

9. It (is) important to improve your sign talk.

10. The trees, mountains, flowers, and rivers smell good.

SONGS
"Follow, I Will Follow"
"Burdens Are Lifted"

MEMORY VERSE
"Believe on the Lord Jesus Christ
and you will be saved."—Acts 16:31

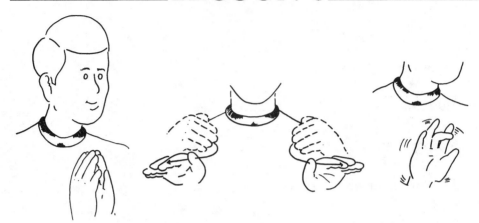

PRAY, ASK

Place hands palm to palm, fingers pointing upward. *Hands together in prayer.*

ANGEL

Place prone hands on shoulders; then move them outward. *Smoothing feathers on the wings.*

MERCY

Wiggle right middle "sensitive" finger, palm outward, up and down several times. *Patting the pitied person on the back.*

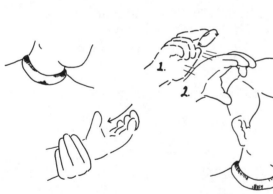

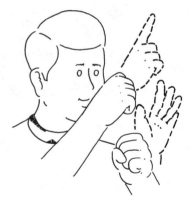

BEG

Move supine hands, fingers pointed outward, in little jerks. *Hands held out in a "wanting" fashion.*

GRACE

Point right "and" fingers downward above the head; open into "five" hand. *Coming from heaven onto the person.*

TRUST

Point right index finger toward heaven, then as hand comes down, both hands grab hold of an imaginary object. *Grab hold of it.*

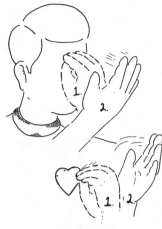

FAITH

Lift right "F" hand toward heaven; bring it down to touch left "F" hand.

GLORY

Rest right prone hand crosswise on left supine hand; move right hand upward with fingers oscillating. *Light radiating upward.*

OBEY

Place "A" hands in front of body, right above the left; open hands into "five" supine hands. *I am at your service.*

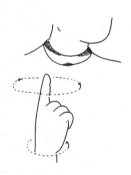

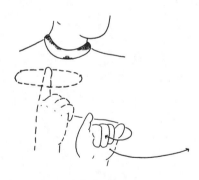

INTERESTING

Place "five" hands in front of face, right hand above left hand; move hands outward away from body; change to "S" hands. *Catches my attention.*

ALWAYS

Make circle with right index finger. *Never ends.*

EVERLASTING

Make circles with right index finger then hand becomes "Y" hand as it pushes outward into future. *Never ending years.*

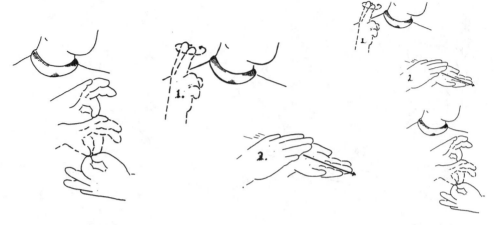

SOUL, SPIRIT

Draw both "F" hands apart at heart but do not touch. *Can't see it or feel it.*

HOLY

Make a circle with right "H" hand in front of body; then move across left supine hand.

HOLY SPIRIT

Make sign for holy and then sign for spirit.

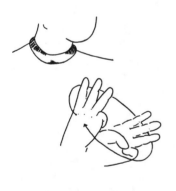

WORLD

Place right "W" hand on left "W" hand; lift right "W" hand and pass it around the left "W" hand. *Around the whole world.*

EARTH

Rest right thumb and middle finger, forming a semicircle, on left "S" hand; move right hand slightly. *Revolving on its axis.*

LAND, DIRT

Rub thumbs and finger-tips of "and" hands together. *Crumbling dirt in planting.*

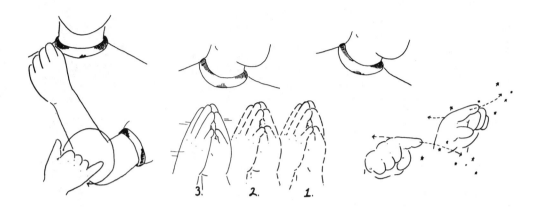

COUNTRY

Hold left arm vertically; move right palm in circles on elbow. *Digging the ground around a tree.*

TOWN, CITY

Make sign for house several times while moving hands from right to left. *Many housetops.*

STARS

Strike "D" hands against one another alternately. *Shooting or twinkling of stars.*

BUILD

Place right palm on back of left hand, then left palm on back of right hand several times. *Placing one brick on top of the other.*

SLEEP

Place "five" hands in front of eyes; close hands to become "and" hands. *Eyes closed.*

DREAM

Move right index finger away from right side of head in a "wavy" pattern. *Thoughts wandering.*

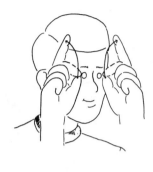

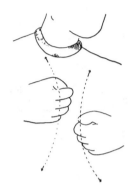

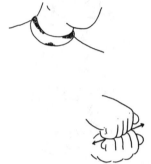

AWAKE

Touch thumb and index finger together at corner of eye; separate thumb and index finger. *Eyes opened.*

BATHE

Move "A" hands alternately up and down on chest. *Scrubbing the body.*

WASH (clothes)

Rub knuckles of right "A" hand against knuckles of left "A" hand. *Scrubbing the clothes.*

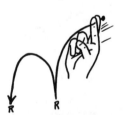

WASH (dishes)

Show circle for plate; then rub right palm over left palm. *Wash the plate.*

COOK

Place right prone hand on left supine hand; then lift and turn over; repeat several times. *Turning the pancakes.*

RESTROOM

Make letter "R" twice, moving from left to right.

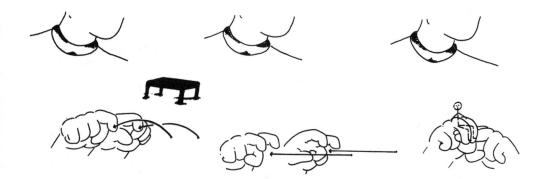

TABLE

With "X" fingers, palms downward, point first to two legs of table; then move towards body to show other two legs of table.

SELFISH, GREEDY

Draw hooked "V" fingers toward body. *Grabbing all for self.*

CHAIR

Left "H" fingers represent the seat of a chair; hang "V" fingers of right hand over left "H" fingers. *Legs hanging down.*

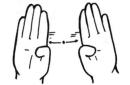

BED

Place "prayer" hand at right side of head. *Head on a pillow.*

DOOR

Place hands side-by-side, palms facing outward. Right hand turns away from left hand. *Show double doors.*

OPEN DOOR

Starting with "door" position, show both hands opening.

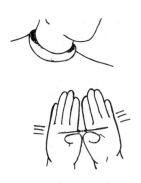

CLOSE DOOR

Show both hands closing; return hands to "door" position.

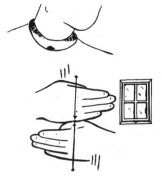

WINDOW

Palms toward body, rest edge of right hand on edge of left hand. *Forming two parts of a window.*

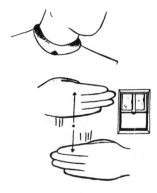

OPEN

Place hands in "window" position then raise right hand slightly off left hand.

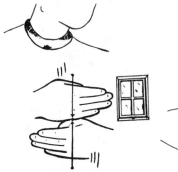

CLOSE

Start with "open" position; return to "window" position.

FENCE

Interlace fingers of horizontal hands, palms inward, then draw hands apart to sides. *Fingers show the rails of the fence.*

JAIL

Place fingers of open hands crosswise before the face, palms inward. *Show bars in front of face.*

FORK

Stick tips of right "W" fingers into the back of left "S" hand. *Sticking prongs into a potato.*

KNIFE

Cut across left index finger with right index finger. *Show whittling.*

SPOON

Dip right cupped "H" fingers into left supine palm. *Dipping the gravy.*

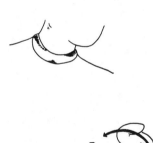

DISH

Show the round shape of a plate with both hands; thumbs and middle fingers not quite touching. *Roundness of plate.*

BONE

Right index finger points to teeth with striking motion. *Teeth are hard and white like bone.*

ROCK

Hit right "A" hand against wrist of left "S" hand several times. *Hard, can't be broken.*

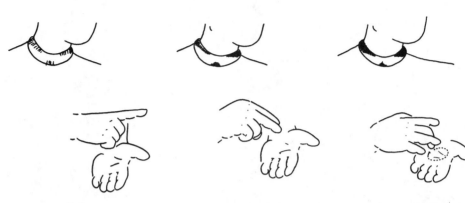

DOCTOR

Place "D" hand on wrist of supine left hand. *Letter "D" used for doctor.*

NURSE

Place "N" on wrist of left supine hand. *Nurse taking pulse.*

MEDICINE

Middle "sensitive" finger of right hand makes circular motion in palm of open supine left hand. *Mixing the medicine.*

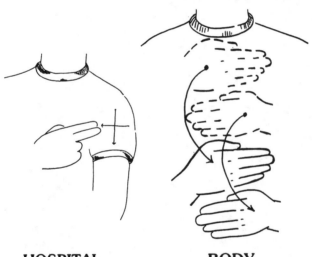

HOSPITAL

Draw a cross with right "H" hand just below left shoulder on arm. *Stands for Red Cross.*

BODY

Place "five" hands, palms inward, on upper part of body and then on lower trunk. *Entire torso.*

WEAK

Stand right inverted "V" fingers in left palm; then bend fingers at knuckles. *Weak knees.*

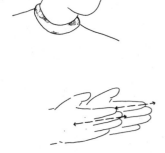

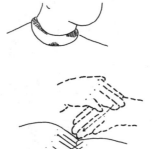

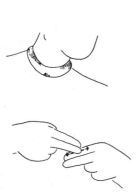

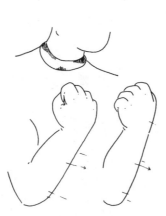

ANXIOUS, EAGER

Rub hands, palm to palm and fingers pointing outward, back and forth vigorously. *Rubbing hands in anticipation.*

COMFORTABLE

Rub right palm across back of left hand and then left palm across back of right hand. *Soothing and consoling.*

TALL

Push right vertical index finger up palm of left vertical hand. *Boy standing against wall to see growth.*

SHORT

Rub right "H" fingers lightly against left "H" fingers. *Just a little bit.*

STRONG, COURAGE, BRAVE

Bring both "five" hands from in front of shoulders forward with emphasis into closed "S" hands. *Strength of arm muscles.*

POWER

Clench fist and make a muscle with left arm; right "C" hand shows height of muscle by making a circle over muscle of left arm. *Strong muscles shown.*

97

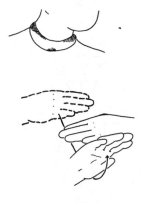

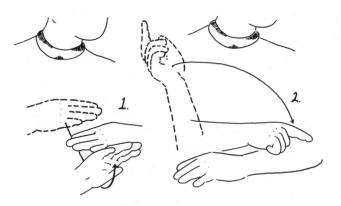

BIRTH

With left arm prone, horizontal before body, move right prone hand down and under left arm. *Child coming from body.*

BIRTHDAY

Make sign for "birth"; then sign for "day."

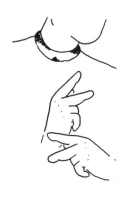

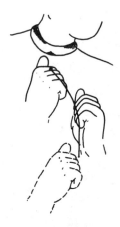

WELL, HEALTHY

Use sign for "strong." *Body is strong.*

KEEP, CARE

Place right "V" hand on top of thumb of left "V" hand. *Eyes are watching.*

MOST

Knuckles of right "A" hand strike hard with upward motion on knuckles of left "A" hand. This is also used for suffix "est." *More added.*

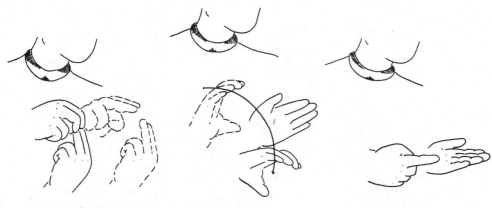

BORROW

Draw left "H" fingers toward body with right hand. *Get from another.*

CHEAP

Strike edge of right prone hand against palm of left hand. *Money thrown away.*

DEBT

Touch tip of right index finger to left supine palm several times. *Money that ought to be paid.*

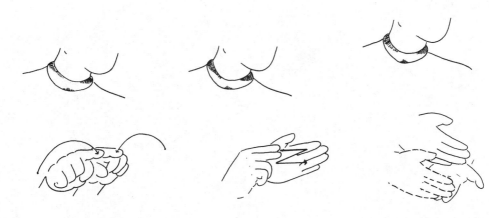

HAPPEN

Turn index fingers, palm toward palm, suddenly inward toward one another. *Falls out.*

READ

Move right "V" fingers down length of left prone hand from tips of fingers to heel of hand without touching. *Eyes scan page.*

LESSON

Place right palm edgewise on left supine palm at two places. *Part to be studied on page.*

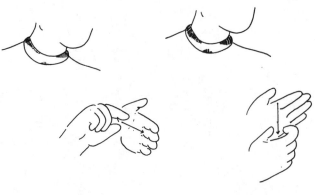

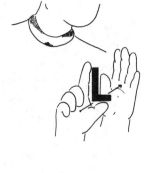

VERSE

Draw thumb and index finger of right hand along left vertical palm from heel of hand to tip of middle finger. *Measure off one verse in palm of hand.*

CHAPTER

Move right "C" hand across left palm.

LAW

Place right "L" against left vertical palm, hand facing outward. *Letter "L" placed on the page of book.*

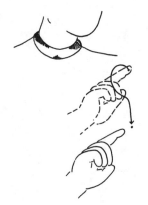

COMMANDMENT

Place right "C" against left vertical palm, hand facing outward. *Letter "C" placed on the tablets.*

QUESTION

Right index finger makes a question mark in front of face. *Question mark made in the air.*

REASON

Move right "R" fingers in circular motion, counter clockwise, in front of forehead. *Letter "R" used to show brains are working.*

FOOL

Place the right index finger and thumb on the nose and give it a sharp pull downward. *Led by the nose.*

FOOLISH

Shake right vertical "Y" hand several times in front of face. *Brains are revolving.*

DIE

Place hands, palm to palm; then turn both hands over. *Face turned up.*

 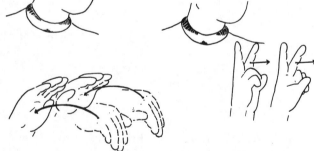

BURY

Move right "H" hand down along side left hand from thumb to heel of hand. *Casket lowered into grave.*

GRAVE

Draw prone hands toward body as if covering the length of the grave; hands become bent. *Covering a grave.*

FUNERAL

Right "V" fingers follow left "V" fingers. *Funeral procession.*

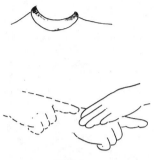

KILL

Thrust right index finger under left prone palm. *Stabbing through.*

CARELESS

Shake right "V" hand from right to left before eyes. *Sight and mind confused.*

SURPRISE, ASTONISH

Join index fingers and thumbs together near temples and then suddenly open and raise index fingers. *The eyes are made to open wide.*

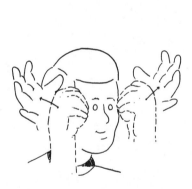

DANGER

Place tips of "and" hands at side of temples; open hands quickly. *Great surprise.*

THIN

Press right thumb and index finger into cheeks to show they are hollow. Or, raise right "F" hand up from left "F" hand to show a long narrow pole. *Hollow cheeked or like a pole.*

FAT

Indicate fat cheeks by holding open bent hands before cheeks, palms inward. Or, move right "Y" hand away from body, oscillating from thumb to little finger. *Swollen cheeks or the wobbling of a fat person walking.*

GUESS

Move right "C" hand across forehead from right to left; change to "S" hand. *Trying to find right answer.*

JOIN

Hook right thumb and index finger onto left thumb and index finger. *Fingers interlocked or joined.*

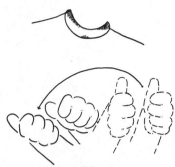

BAPTIZE, BAPTISM

"A" hands face one another; right "A" hand becomes supine; left "A" hand becomes prone; return hands to original position. *Dip into water.*

BAPTIST

Move "B" hand in clockwise circle; then make sign for "baptism."

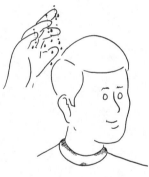

METHODIST

Hold right "O" hand over head; open into "five" hand; repeat several times. *Sprinkling on head.*

LUTHERAN

Place tip of thumb of right "L" hand on left elbow.

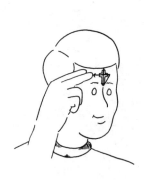

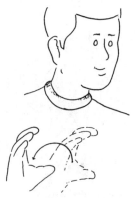

CATHOLIC

Fingertips of right "H" hand, palm inward, trace a cross at forehead.

CHURCH OF CHRIST

Move right "C" hand from left to right.

LESSON 5 PRACTICE

1. Always pray to God for everything.

2. This medicine made his body weak.

3. Study the laws and commandments.

4. Ask questions of interest and always learn.

5. Dirt in country is good for growing flowers.

6. Everlasting life is for all saved people.

7. Angels watch us here on earth.

8. Cook good food and leave on table.

9. Doctors and nurses work in hospital.

10. The strong doctor was tall and fat.

SONGS
"Every Day With Jesus"
"Thank You Lord"

MEMORY VERSE
"For God so loved the world [people] that He gave His only [born] Son that all who believe in [Jesus] shall not perish but have everlasting life."—John 3:16.

LESSON 6

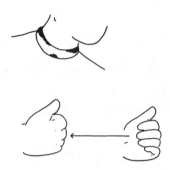

PROMISE

Point right index finger at lips, then bring right prone hand down and place it on top of left "S" hand. *Speak and seal.*

JEALOUS

Place tip of small finger of right hand on right jaw then bring hand forward and trace the letter "J" in the air.

BACKSLIDE

Move right "A" hand toward body from left "A" hand. *Going backwards.*

SPOIL

Rub right prone hand across back of left prone hand as if petting an animal. *Too much petting.*

FEW

Draw tip of right thumb across the tips of fingers from index to little finger. *So few you can count them on your fingers.*

ROAD

"R" hands trace outline of road as they move outward from body.

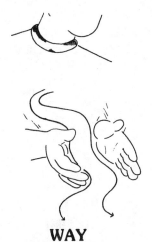

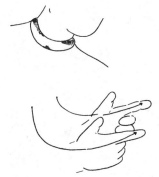

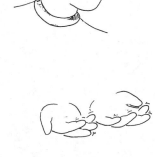

WAY

Draw "W" hands outward from body. *Letter "W" used to show outline of road.*

LET

Move "L" hands, palm to palm, away from body.

WAIT

Wiggle fingers of "five" hands with palms toward body and fingers pointing up. *Hands beckoning not to go.*

VISIT

With "V" hands, palm to palm, fingers pointing up, move hands toward and away from each other. *Two people talking.*

LETTER

Take thumb tip of right "A" hand from lip to index finger of left supine hand. *Licking stamp and placing it on envelope.*

WRITE

Tips of right thumb and index finger join together and write on left palm.

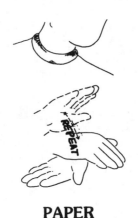

STAMP

Touch right "H" hand to lips and then place on left supine hand. *Lick stamp and put on letter.*

PAPER

Hit heel of right prone hand against heel of left supine hand. *Pressing to print.*

ALONE

Move right "D" finger, palm inward, in a circle. *One standing alone.*

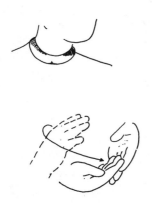

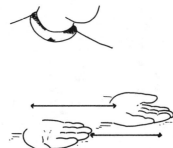

ARRIVE

Move right bent hand clockwise and then rest it on left palm. *Right hand travels and arrives.*

SERVE

Move supine hands back and forth alternately. *Carrying a tray.*

KISS

Place right "and" hand at mouth; then move it to the cheek. *From lips to cheek.*

FLAG, BANNER

Place right elbow in left palm; wave right hand. *Flag atop flagpole waving in the breeze.*

WIN

Wave right "A" hand around and above head. *Victorious person waving a flag.*

NOTICE

Point to eye and then to left supine palm with right index finger. *Eye sees object or something on page.*

LIP-READ

Move right "R" hand counterclockwise around the lips.

MOVE, TRANSFER

Place prone hands at left side of body; grasp something with "and" hands and lift imaginary object up and over and down to the right side of body. *Pick up, carry, and put down.*

AUTO, DRIVE

Both hands grasp at an imaginary steering wheel and turn it from side to side. *Steering an automobile.*

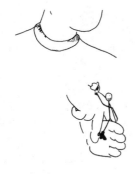

RIDE (on horse)

Right inverted "V" fingers straddle left "H" hand; move hands to represent the gallup of horse with rider. *Legs astride a horse.*

RIDE (in car)

Hang fingers of right "H" hand over thumb of left "C" hand.

TRAIN

Move right "H" fingers back and forth on left "H" fingers; both hands prone. *Train on tracks.*

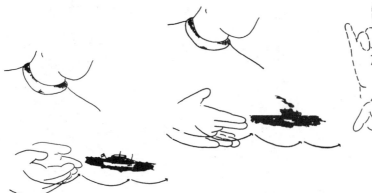

BOAT

With hands together, form shape of boat; move hands forward to show motion over the waves. *Boat tossing on waves.*

SHIP

Hold right "three" hand, fingers pointing forward to show smokestack of ship; move forward away from body to show rocking motion of the ship. *Ship tossing on waves.*

AIRPLANE

Right "Y" hand, with index finger extended to show wings and nose, moves outward and away from body. *Plane flying.*

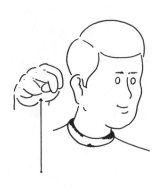

TELEPHONE

Position right "Y" hand with little finger at lips and thumb at ear. *Talking on the phone.*

NORTH

Raise right "N" hand up to show northern regions on map.

SOUTH

Move right "S" hand down to show southern regions on map.

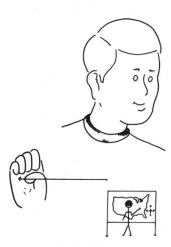

EAST

Move right "E" hand to right of body to show eastern regions on map.

WEST

Move right "W" hand to left side of body to show western regions on map.

HOPE

Oscillate bent tandem hands. *Thoughts are wavering.*

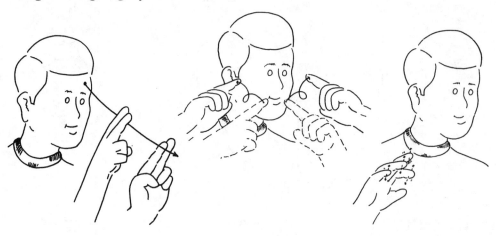

HONOR

Lower right vertical "H" hand and then move it forward. *Gesture of respect.*

FAMOUS

Move right index finger forward in a spiraling fashion from lips. *Told abroad.*

SPELL

Wiggle fingers of right prone hand as hand is moved from left to right. *Speaking by spelling.*

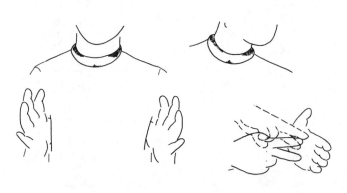

VACATION, IDLE

Place thumbs under imaginary suspenders and wiggle fingers. *Men standing around with thumbs under suspenders.*

MEANING

Twist right "V" fingers on supine palm of left hand. *Unwinding the tangles.*

IDEA

Place tip of "I" finger of right hand on cheek just below the eye; then move hand forward and upward with a jerk. *A little thought just sprung up.*

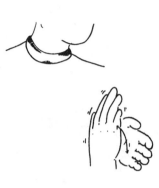

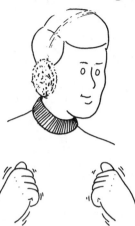

PICTURE

Move right "C" hand from side of face to vertical left palm. *Picture of face put on paper.*

MOVIE

Shake right prone "five" hand over left supine "five" hand. *Flickering of the light on the screen.*

WINTER

Shake "S" hands in front of chest. *Shivering from cold.*

SUMMER

Draw right "X" hand across the forehead from left to right; then shake the hand. *Wiping drops of sweat from forehead.*

SPRING

Push right "and" hand up through left "O" hand with quick jerks. *Things growing.*

AUTUMN

Point left arm upward and push right prone "V" hand down along the sides of arm. *Leaves falling from tree.*

113

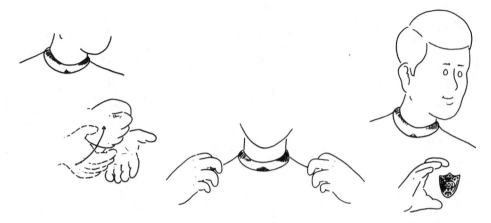

EARN, REAP

Draw right bent hand, palm leftward, across left supine palm several times. *Scraping up all the money.*

BOSS, CAPTAIN

Place cupped hands on shoulders; lift and change to "and" hands. *Epaulets on the shoulders.*

POLICEMAN

Place right "C" hand just beneath left shoulder. *Use "C" for "Cop"*

FARM

Move tip of thumb of right "five" hand across the chin from left to right. *Ploughing the land.*

FARMER

Use sign for "farm" and then sign for "er."

ROBBER

Draw right "N" hand from middle of lip rightward and left "N" hand from middle of lip leftward. *Mask on face.*

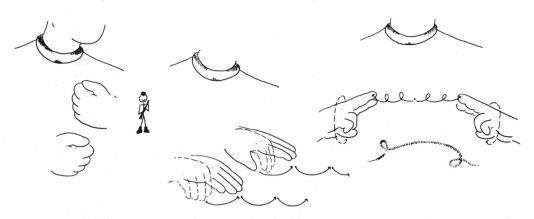

SOLDIER

Position "A" hands as if holding a gun. *Soldier holding gun.*

MARCH, PARADE

Move tandem "four" hands away from body; move fingers in marching fashion. *Legs of soldiers marching in step.*

ROPE

Touch finger tips of "R" hands; then pull hands apart in a spiral pattern.

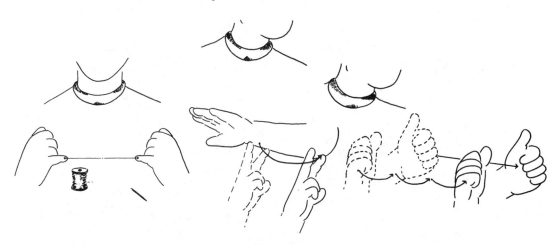

THREAD, STRING

Point left "I" hand to right; touch tips of right "I" and left "I" fingers; then pull toward right. *Pulling thread off spool.*

BRIDGE

Place right "V" fingers first beneath the wrist and then beneath the elbow of left horizontal prone arm. *Four bridge supports shown.*

GUIDE

Right "A" hand follows left "A" hand; move hand away from body. *One person follows the leader.*

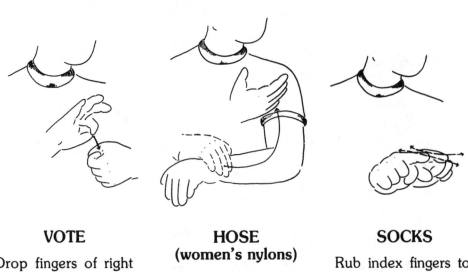

VOTE

Drop fingers of right "F" hand into left "O" hand. *Drop into the ballot box.*

HOSE
(women's nylons)

Pull right prone hand across back of left prone arm from hand toward shoulder. *Pulling on hose.*

SOCKS

Rub index fingers together several times. *Socks being pulled on.*

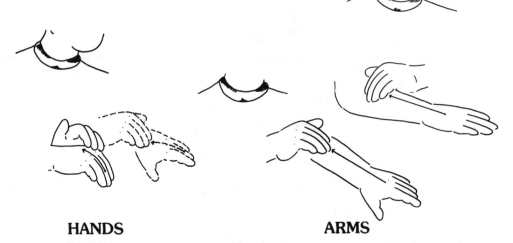

HANDS

Rub back of left prone hand with right prone hand. Then rub back of right prone hand with left prone hand. *Rubbing hands.*

ARMS

Rub left prone arm with right prone hand; rub right prone arm with left prone hand. *Rubbing arms.*

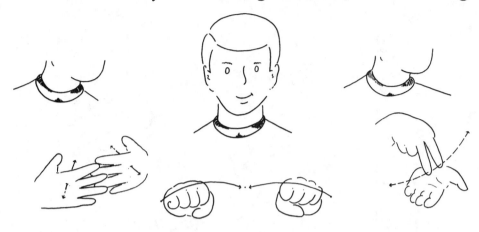

FEET

Pass fingers of right prone hand in between fingers of left prone hand several times. *Fingers represent toes.*

SHOES

Bring "S" hands together in front of body. *Making of shoes.*

DANCE

Swing right inverted "V" hand over left supine palm. *Feet swaying to and fro.*

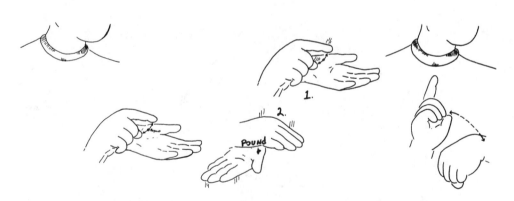

PRINT

Pick typefaces from font with right thumb and index finger and place them in left supine hand. *Printer setting up type in old-fashioned way.*

NEWSPAPER

Use sign for print then sign for paper. *The printed paper.*

DUTY

Hit right "D" hand against wrist of left "S" hand.

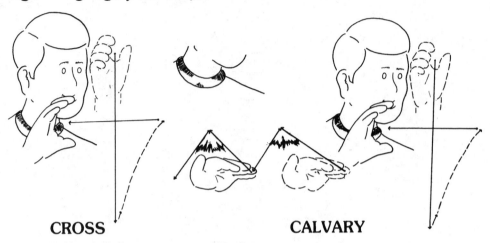

CROSS

Trace the horizontal then the vertical beams of the cross with right "C" hand. *Beams of the cross.*

CALVARY

Make sign for mountain, then sign for cross. *Mountain and cross.*

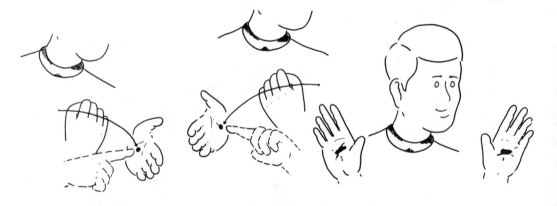

CRUCIFY

Place tip of right index finger on left palm and strike palm with fist; then place tip of left index finger on right palm and strike palm with fist; hold hands outstretched. *Nailing hands to cross.*

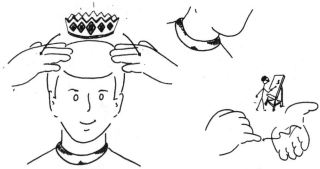

PRIEST

Draw thumb and index finger of each hand from center of neck to shoulders. *Collar worn by priest.*

CROWN

Form circle with hands in front of body; then move hands upward and place on head. *Crown placed on head.*

DRAW

Draw with right "I" little finger on left supine palm. *Tracing the drawing.*

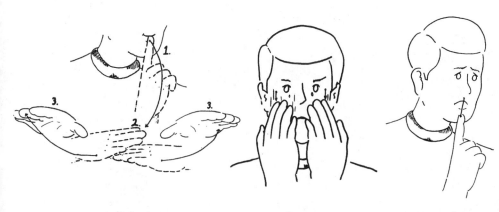

CALM

Place right index finger against mouth; then bring both prone hands down and out with right hand going rightward and left hand going leftward. *Showing waves are stilled.*

SAD

Place palms of both "five" hands in front of the face; move hands downward slightly as head bows. *Face buried in hands.*

LONESOME

With right index finger pointing upward in front of the face, move it slightly back and forth. *All alone.*

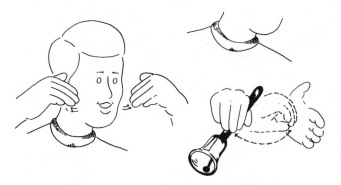
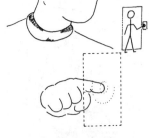
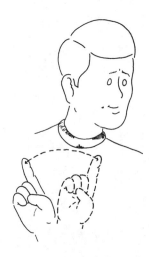

LAUGH

Draw both "4" hands away from corners of the mouth. *Wrinkles caused by laughter.*

BELL

Grasp the bell and ring it or grasp the rope to ring the bell. *Motion made in the ringing of any bell, according to its kind.*

DOORBELL

Punch imaginary button of doorbell.

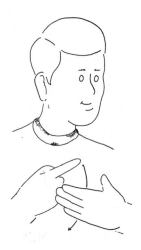

WHAT

Point to left supine palm with tip of right index finger. *Asking, "What is on that page?"*

SOME

Edge of right hand cuts across palm of left supine hand from thumb to heel of hand. *Cutting off a portion.*

WHERE

Move right index finger back and forth several times. *N. S. for "where?"*

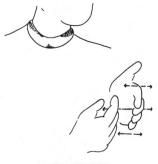

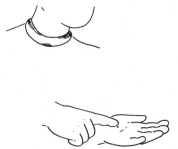

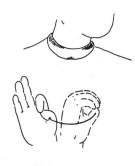

DOESN'T MATTER ANYWAY

Hit tips of right fingers hard against tips of left fingers with a downward motion. Then bring right hand back up, striking the left fingertips again (both hands prone).

THIS

Point right index finger at something in left supine palm. *Something near.*

OF

Combine letters "O" and "F" into one gesture.

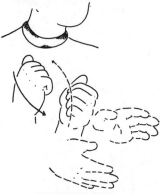

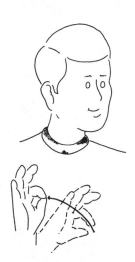

DESTROY

Move right "five" hand across left "five" hand with force; change to "S" hands; return to first position, becoming "five" hands. *Tearing asunder.*

PICK, CHOOSE

Reach out and close together right index finger and thumb. *Picking up something.*

DIRTY

Wiggle fingers of right prone hand under chin. (Same sign used for "pig.")

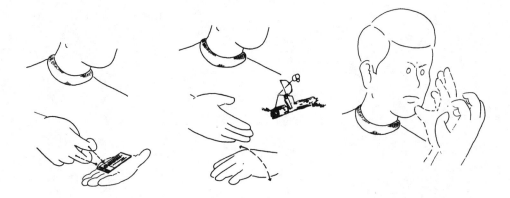

TICKET

Place bent "V" fingers of right hand on edge of left hand. *Punching the ticket.*

WOOD

Use edge of right hand to "saw" index finger of left prone hand.

MAD

Bring right "five" hand, palm towards face, forward to become "and" hand. *Face contorted.*

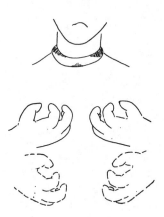

ANGER

Bring bent fingers of "five" hands upward on body. *Boiling in body.*

LESSON 6 PRACTICE

1. Wait (and) visit with (the) teacher.

2. You get paper (and) stamp (to) write your mother (a) letter.

3. Notice (the) flag (on the) house.

4. The movie showed pictures of summertime.

5. He (is a) guide and earned much money.

6. Jesus (was) crucified (on) cross (on) Calvary.

7. Draw (the) picture (to) print (in) newspaper.

8. (The) soldiers marched through (the) farm.

9. (The) flag arrived on train, not on airplane.

10. What (do) you mean (to) vote for bad man?

SONGS
"Nothing But the Blood"
"More, More About Jesus"

MEMORY VERSE
"There is none good, no not one."—Romans 3:10.

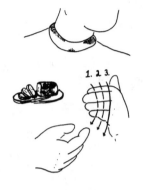  

BREAD

Cut across back of left hand, palm facing body, with fingertips of right hand. *Slicing of the bread.*

BUTTER

Move right "H" fingers down left supine palm from middle finger to heel of hand. *Spreading butter on bread.*

MILK

Squeeze "S" hands alternately. *Milking a cow.*

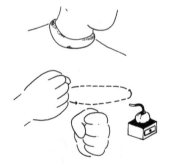 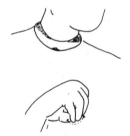 

COFFEE

Move right "S" hand clockwise on left "S" hand. *Grinding in coffee mill.*

SUGAR

Rub thumb against fingers of right "O" hand. *Sprinkling sugar on food.*

SALT

Bring right "H" fingers to lips, palm inward; then to back of left "H" fingers. *Taste and then put on food.*

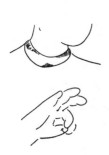

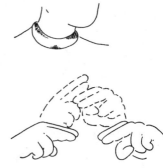

PEPPER

Shake "F" hand with fingers pointing down. *Shake pepper from the shaker.*

TEA

Move right "F" hand around left "O" hand. *Stirring the tea bag in the cup.*

EGGS

Strike right "H" hand against left "H" hand; then separate hands with a downward semi-circle movement. *Breaking eggs open.*

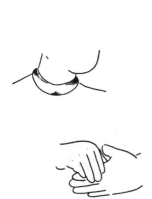

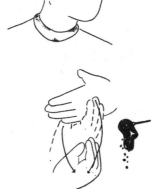

MEAT

With index finger and thumb of right hand, take hold of left hand between thumb and index finger. *Grab the meaty part of hand.*

GRAVY

With fingers of right hand and thumb, take hold of lower edge of left hand and pull downward (left hand facing body). *Drips from meat.*

FISH

Move right hand, palm toward left, forward with a wriggling motion. *Motion of hand shows wriggling of fish.*

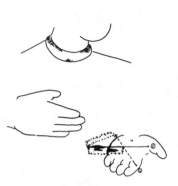

PIE

Outline a slice of pie with edge of right hand on left supine palm. *Cutting wedged-shaped pieces.*

CAKE

Bring right "C" hand down from chin, palm inward. *Crumbs falling from mouth.*

CANDY

Place tip of right index finger at corner of mouth. *Stick of candy in mouth.*

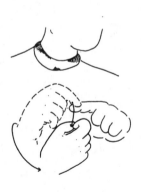

BEANS

With index finger and thumb of right hand, snap tip of index finger of left hand. *Snapping beans.*

CORN

Rake right "C" hand downward on elbow of left vertical arm; left hand forms "S." *Shelling corn.*

APPLE

Press knuckle of index finger of right "S" hand sharply into right cheek. *Shows depression around stem of apple.*

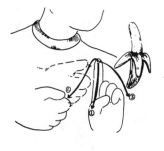   

BANANA

Hold left index finger vertically to represent a banana; "peel" with right hand. *Peeling a banana.*

PEACH

Bring right hand down cheek and form "and" hand. *Fuzz on cheek represents fuzz on peach.*

WATERMELON

Thump back of left "S" hand with right middle finger. *Thump for ripeness.*

TOMATOES

Point to lips with tip of right index finger; then slice across left "and" hand. *Slicing red tomatoes.*

SYRUP

Move right "H" hand, palm facing inward, up and down on right cheek. *Spreading syrup.*

GUM

Twist right index finger into right cheek. *Stuck in jaw.*

BEER

Hold thumbtip of right "Y" hand to lips. *Tilting the bottle.*

WHISKEY

Place right index finger and little finger of right hand on back of left "S" hand. *Measuring of a fifth.*

WINE

With tip of right index finger of "W" hand make a circle on cheek, palm leftward. *Rosy color of wine.*

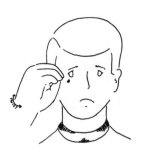

ONION

Twist tips of right "and" hand at corner of the eye. *Tears caused by peeling.*

CABBAGE

Place both "five" hands at sides of head. *Shows leaves of head of cabbage.*

CHEESE

Press heels of hands together. *Pressing water from cheese.*

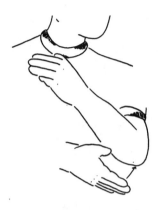

CRACKERS

Crack left elbow several times with right "five" hand.

NUT

Place thumbtip of right "A" hand between the teeth. *Cracking a nut with the teeth.*

RED

Point to lips with right index finger. *Lips are red.*

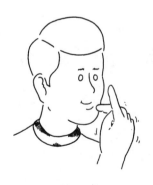

PINK

Bring middle finger of right "P" hand down across lip.

BLACK

Rub tip of right index finger across eyebrows from left to the right. *Dark eyebrows.*

BROWN

Draw right "B" hand down cheek near hair. *Long brown hair.*

129

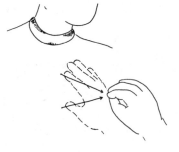

WHITE

Lay open palm of right "five" hand on chest, then draw outward, changing to "and" fingers. *White bib worn by nuns.*

PURPLE

Shake "P" hand in front of body.

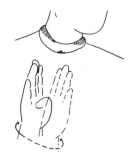

BLUE

Shake "B" hand in front of body.

GREEN

Shake "G" hand in front of body.

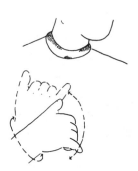

YELLOW

Shake "Y" hand in front of body.

MONDAY

Make circular motion with "M" hand in front of body.

TUESDAY

Make circular motion with "T" hand in front of body.

WEDNESDAY

Make circular motion with "W" hand in front of body.

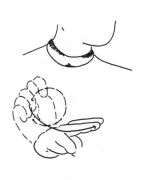

THURSDAY

Make circular motion with combination of "T" and "H" hands in front of body.

FRIDAY

Make circular motion with "F" hand in front of body.

SATURDAY

Make circular motion with "S" hand in front of body.

SUNDAY

Spread vertical hands, palms outward, apart to indicate doors opening. *Large open doors of church building.*

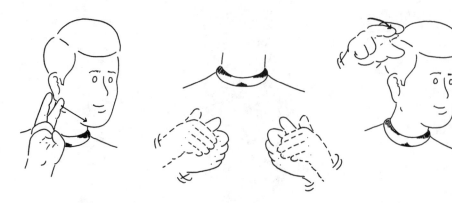

VIRGIN

Shake "V" hand at chin.

ANIMALS

Place fingertips of each hand beneath armpits; move elbows in and out. *Show breathing of an animal.*

HORSE

Place right "V" hand at side of head to represent an ear. *Upright ears of horse.*

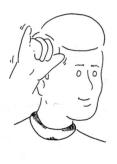

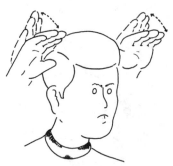

COW

Place tip of thumb of right "Y" hand against side of forehead. *Horns of a cow.*

DONKEY

Place both "five" hands at sides of head to represent large ears. *Large, upright ears.*

STUBBORN

Use sign for donkey.

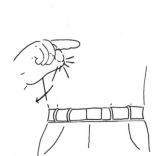

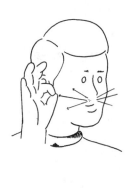

PIG

Make sign for "full" and then sign for "dirty." *Eats a great deal and is dirty.*

DOG

Snap middle finger and thumb of right hand. *Calling the dog.*

CAT

Draw tip of index finger and thumb of right hand from side of mouth. *Pulling at the whiskers of a cat.*

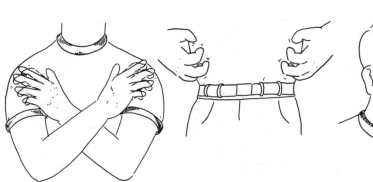

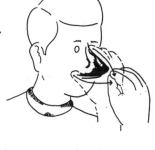

BEAR

Cross arms on breast and scratch arms with fingers near the shoulder. *Show a bear standing and performing.*

MONKEY

Scratch upward with bent hands at bottom of ribs. *Monkey scratching himself.*

WOLF

Draw right "five" hand away from nose and changed to "and" hand. *Pointed nose of the wolf.*

FOX

Twist right "F" hand in front of nose. *Nose of fox.*

BIRD, CHICKEN

Join thumb and index finger together and place in front of lips; lift index finger off of thumb. *Beak of bird pecking.*

BEE

Pinch right cheek with index finger and thumb of right hand. *A bee stinging.*

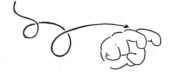

LION

Move bent fingers of right hand over top of head to represent a lion's mane. *The bushy mane of a lion.*

SNAKE

Move right "B" fingers and arm outward from body in a wriggling fashion. *Snake wriggling away.*

WORM

Left hand held edgewise. Index finger of right hand wriggles as it is pushed on the left palm. *Worm wriggling on wall.*

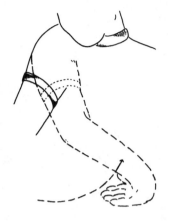 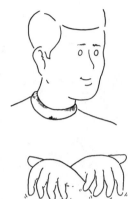 

ELEPHANT

Extend right arm from nose and swing arm from side to side. *Elephant's trunk.*

SPIDER

Cross prone hand at wrists; move fingers like legs. *Legs of spider.*

BUG

Walk right curved "five" hand over the back of left prone hand. *Bug crawling over back of hand.*

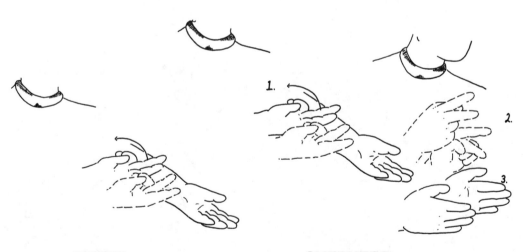

SHEEP

Face left supine arm and hand away from body; using right "V" hand as scissors, move up left arm. *Shearing wool from back of sheep.*

SHEPHERD

Make sign for "sheep"; then sign for "keeper." *Sheep keeper.*

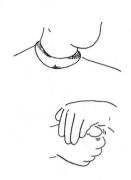

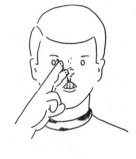

TURTLE

Place right "A" hand under left prone hand. *Head sticks out from beneath shell.*

RAT, MOUSE

Rub the right "R" hand down the bridge of the nose. *Wrinkling nose of a mouse.*

FROG

Flick right "V" fingers under chin upward. *Croaking of frog in throat.*

DEER

Place both "five" hands at temples. *Antlers shown.*

GOAT

Put right "S" hand at chin for whiskers then right "V" fingers at forehead for horns. *Whiskers and horns shown.*

AMERICA

Interlock fingers; then move in a circular motion from right to left. *All states united.*

Instructions for Converting Individual Words into Signs

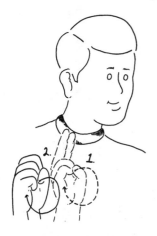

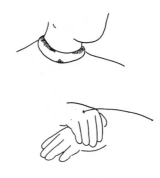

UNITED STATES

Place right "U" fingers, then right "S" fingers in front of body.

EUROPE

Right "E" hand, palm inward, circled around the face counter-clockwise. *Facial features of Europeans.*

ENGLAND

Grab left hand with right hand and give a good shake. *The English are considered great handshakers.*

FRANCE

Move vertical right arm with "F" hand back and forth. *A flag waving.*

ITALY

Trace a cross with tip of right "I" finger on the forehead, palm inward. *Catholic Italy.*

GERMANY

Cross hands held edgewise at wrists before face, fingers oscillating. *Crossed flags on coat of arms.*

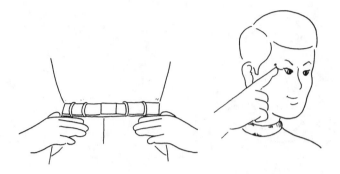

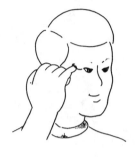

RUSSIA

Rest hands, palms downward, on hips. *Armor worn to protect hips.*

CHINA

With right index finger, push up corner of eye. *Slanted eyes of Orientals.*

JAPAN

With right "I" finger, push up corner of eye *Slanted eyes of Orientals.*

AFRICA

Draw thumb of "A" hand across forehead.

INDIANS

Draw tips of joined index finger and thumb of right hand up cheek from lips to ear. *Painted streak up side of face.*

JEWS

Place right "C" hand on chin; then close to become "S" hand. *Pull on goatee.*

138

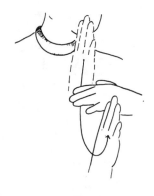 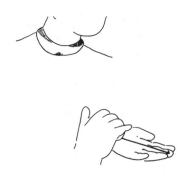 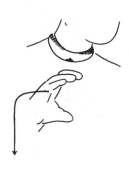

HUMBLE

Bring right "B" hand from lips down under left prone hand. *Shows willingness to be under authority.*

NEW YORK

Slide right "Y" hand along left supine palm.

CHICAGO

Hold right arm vertically; wave right "C" hand back and forth as a flag.

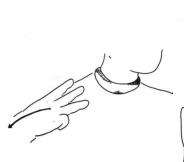  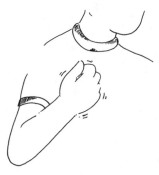

WASHINGTON

Draw right "W" hand downward from head, behind ear, in a wavy line. *Letter "W" used and curly locks shown, as worn in the days of Washington.*

CALIFORNIA

Point to earlobe with right index finger, then change to "Y" hand as hand turns away from ear. *Earrings made from gold found in the early days of California.*

CANADA

Grasp lapel of coat with right "A" hand. *Lapel of coat worn by Royal Mounted Canadian Police.*

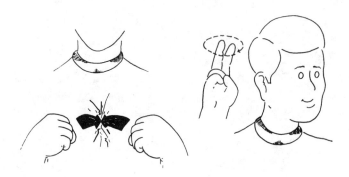

COLLIDE, WRECK

Ram right "S" hand into left "S" hand. *Two vehicles ramming into one another.*

VICTORY

Move vertical right arm with "V" fingers from right to left. *Flag waving.*

LESSON 7 PRACTICE

1. You get bread, butter, (and) coffee (to) eat.

2. The pig, cow, horse, dog, (and) cat live on farm.

3. You cut (the) pie and you get (the) coffee (to) serve.

4. Candy (and) apples (are) good together.

5. Whiskey, wine, (and) beer hurt your body.

6. Monday, Wednesday, (and) Saturday you must have black on.

7. (The) bird (was) red with brown on (his) back.

8. (The) Indians live in New York and won't work.

9. The Jews (people) worship on Friday and Saturday (and) work hard.

10. America and England (are) good friends.

SONGS
"He Lives"
"Just a Closer Walk"

MEMORY VERSE
"All have sinned and come short of
the glory of God"—Romans 3:23.

LESSON 8

Interpreting Spoken Words Into Signs

Remember: The most important facts of interpreting are:
1. Learn to think deaf.
2. Be sure you are making yourself clear. Do the deaf understand? Are your signs clear, bright, and understandable?
3. It is not important to sign fast. It is more important to get the message across.
4. It is not important to know a multitude of signs, but it is important to know a few well and to use them properly.
5. It is important to use simple, easy language understood by the deaf.
6. Practice, practice, practice makes a good interpreter.

Rules for Interpreting

1. Listen with your eyes. Learn in your head, on your hands, and in your heart! Sign Language is a way of presenting thoughts via pictures made with the hands. So learn to hear the spoken word, but be able to change it into pictures for the eyes of the deaf. This is why it is so important to use your body, your face, and your eyes to convey the message to the deaf.

2. The language of signs should not be bound to the English sentence. In working with the deaf (and certainly if you have deaf children) it would be well to use correct sentence structure to help them learn the proper use of the English language. But in interpreting there is no time for this.

3. Try to wait for a whole sentence or at least enough to be sure you know where the speaker is going and then change into signs. You might get the wrong thought from the first of the sentence. Do not try to translate every English word into a sign.

4. Spell as few words as possible. Deaf find it hard to read spelling the same as you—especially at a distance. If you must spell, look at their faces to be sure they understand your spelling. If there is any doubt, spell it again.

5. Do not use the same sign for two different words in the same sentence. Example: The same sign is used for the word "eat" as for the word "food." If these words are used in the same sentence—"I will eat the good food"—either "eat" or "food" should be spelled. Using the sign "eat" in both instances comes out—"I will eat the eat."

Suggestions and Further Helps for Learning Sign Language

6. Use the very simplest forms of English words. Use words that a three- or four-year-old hearing child could understand.

Example: "I am exhausted"—change to—"I am tired." "Go to the department store"—change to—"Go to the dress store." "He is perplexed"—change to—"He is upset or troubled."

7. Use short, direct sentences.

Example: "Today we will go to town, but we must get the dishes washed, get the clothes ready to wash, and I must call Father before we go." Change to—"Today we must town go. First, we must wash dishes. And then we must get all clothes ready to wash. I must call Father."

8. Be sure to interpret the exact meaning of words—avoid idioms.

A woman said about our deaf daughter's baby son— "Isn't Jimmy cute!" Betty immediately asked why the woman did *not* think her baby cute. The word "isn't" to her meant "is not cute." That would be better interpreted— "I think Jimmy is cute—you agree?"

In speaking of an ill person we might ask, "How did you find your sick friend today?" To the deaf the word "find" would mean searching for a lost sick friend. Better to interpret—"Your sick friend improving?"

In signing Scripture, care must be taken to get the correct meaning. For example, if you sign "Feed (sign for eating) my sheep" the deaf would probably think you mean you are eating lunch. Better to interpret—"Give food (spell) to my sheep."

Examples of idioms:

Actions speak louder than words
At one's wit's end
Bend over backward, lean over backward
Eat humble pie
Food for thought
Get to first base, reach first base
High and dry
Run ragged
Small wonder
Up to snuff

9. Learn to leave out all unnecessary words. Make your interpreting like the wording of a telegram. Example: "Tonight let us turn to the Book of Acts, chapter sixteen, the thirty-first verse."—change to—"Tonight, Bible, Acts 16:31."

10. Often one sign is used for several words. But facial expression can show the degree of intensity of meaning.

Examples:

Jesus *loves* you.
The man spoke *loving* words.
She is my *dear* friend.
His *affection* for the dog is wonderful.

Using the lips as you sign can help the deaf to "see" which word you mean. This is especially important with the younger generation of deaf who have had oral training.

Below are some words that are made by the same sign:

Pretty, lovely, beauty
Love, loving, affection, dear, beloved, darling
Wonderful, precious, magnificent
Worship, adore, admire

11. Sometimes it may take several signs to convey a word.

Examples:

Justify—make right with God
Amazed—feel surprised
Reconciliation—far, together, peace

12. Words spelled alike often have different meanings. Be sure to interpret the meaning.

Examples:

Save—as in save from sin. *Save*—as in save money.
I am *well.* He is in the *well. Well,* where have you been?
Will you go? (Use "maybe" sign.) He made a *will.* We *will* go tomorrow.

13. In interpreting conversations, be sure to shift your position to show the different persons talking. If you are telling the story of the angel talking with Mary, play the part of the angel talking. Then turn to show Mary talking.

14. Constantly observe other interpreters so you can learn ways to improve and to convey the correct meaning of sentences with a few simple signs. Also, observe the errors they make.

Example of a short cut: "Ladies and gentlemen, I am happy to be here. It is a real joy and pleasure to be at the Bill Rice Ranch for this summer camp season." Interpretation: "Women, men. (There is a sign for ladies and gentlemen but it varies from state to state so it is better to use the sign for women and men.) He (point to speaker) happy here. True happy and wonderful arrive Bill Rice Ranch (here spell ranch and then give sign for ranch—"R" on wrist) this summer camp time."

With this you get the entire meaning across but keep up with the speaker. Be sure the important words are given to the deaf. You have a responsibility both to the deaf and to the speaker. You owe it to the deaf to give them the full meaning, but you owe it to the speaker to truthfully tell what he is saying.

Reading Sign Language

It is more difficult to read the deaf as they use signs than to talk to them with signs.

1. Master the signs. Become familiar with them. Talk to the deaf as often as possible to learn to read the signs on another's hands.

2. Practice with someone on spelling. This is the downfall for most of us. As you walk or ride, practice with words you see on signs. As you read your Bible, spell and sign to yourself.

3. Do not be ashamed to ask the deaf to sign more slowly or to repeat. Better to find out exactly what the deaf person is saying than to nod your head "yes" only to discover you have given your assent or agreed to the wrong thing.

Example: I noticed a deaf boy asking his counselor if he could go to his girl friend's room to look at her picture album. The counselor, who was new in signs, was smiling and nodding his head. Fortunately I was nearby and could help out in the situation as boys are not allowed in girls' rooms at our ranch.

4. The deaf often act as if they understand something we have said to them when they really do not.

Example: One Sunday during a baptismal service, a deaf boy went in search of the restroom. One of the deacons saw the boy roaming around and asked him if he wanted to be baptized. The boy grinned and nodded his head. He was immediately ushered into a room, given a robe, and brought to the baptistry. The preacher thought he had baptized this boy previously, but this was no time for questions, so he went ahead and baptized him.

Afterward it was learned the boy had not understood the deacon's signs, but to be agreeable he had nodded his head affirmatively. So, the boy was baptized twice.

5. The only way to understand the deaf is to learn "deaf talk" and to feel deaf. Watch them as they talk to one another and see how they express themselves.

Example: Often deaf will say for "I was absent"—"I empty." Or asked if they have been to Georgia they will say, "I never touched on Georgia. You touched Georgia?" You will notice if a deaf person is asked if they have done something such as ridden a horse, or eaten their dinner, or gone to town they may answer with the "late" sign, meaning they are behind and have not gotten it done. "He tease on me!" is used to explain a teasing fellow.

6. Learn to extract the meaning from what you see. Forget English sentence structure and try to get the idea of what is being signed.

7. Watch for the whole thought and then translate it into what is being said.

Example: If a deaf person signs, "Boy, town finish go" then you will know he said, "The boy has already gone to town." "The mother house mad on me" means "The house mother is mad at me."

Letters from the Deaf

These letters will give you an idea of how the deaf communicate:

Dear Folks,

How are you? I am fine.

I am sorry that I will not be camp this year because I have new job. I working printing at Continental Insurance Company at Chicago.

Tell someone and have nice fun around of camp. Keep God bless you.

I love God and everyone because nothing wrong and harms of people.

Tell Bill hello and how are you?

See you next year. Sincerely, (Signed) Jack

Dear Mrs. Catherine Rice,

I am Doris' best friend. I want to tell you something. Doris and I might go to Bill Rice Ranch Camp. I want you to file Millie Russo, Doris Melton, Debra, and me at same room. Will you do for me? I hope I can go there this summer.

Cathy, please list the kind of clothes that I can bring them.
Will you please to answer me back. I'll send you my home address.
Your truly, (Signed) Sharon
P.S. Hope I can go there.

Dearest Mother,

Jimmy was so happy be home and he was sleep good. I was so happy to see you again.

Don's mother called Dr. Smiley and he said that too much walk and too much salt so he sent me a pills. It help me much better now. Next Tuesday I will be six weeks so I will go to doctor and on Thursday Jimmy will go to doctor, too.

I was surprised Milton and Ronnie came to see me and Jimmy while Don work. They went to Ga. and Fla. Milton said that he was enjoyed in different states school for the deaf.

Yes, I received the package for Jimmy from Sunday School. I will write to them.

Just forget it we didn't tell Dad about car. When we arrived here from Murfreesboro the car was broke through gasket. We will try to buy new motor. Please pray for us if the Lord's will to buy a new car or keep it. (old car)

Don wrote to Harvey Springer about 2 times but we never hear from him. He will write to New York. We must know what dates for Colorado and New York.

Last Tuesday Jimmy was first time to eat cereal and he like it. He weighed 10 lb. and 22 inch.

Don's mother and dad brought a baby seat for Jimmy.

I kiss Jimmy for you.

With all love,
(Signed) Betty, Don & Jimmy, Dollie & Fluffy

LESSON 9

Helpful Ways to Remember Signs

Learn to forget:

1. *That you can hear.* This is very difficult to do because hearing is the last of the five senses to leave us as we drop off to sleep but the first to return to us as we begin to wake up. Deaf feel sound through their bodies and feet. If there is a loud noise they might put their hands over their ears and say "loud," but they feel it rather than hear it. I have seen Betty sitting in church holding onto a song book because she could "feel" music through the book.

When Betty was small, my husband's brother was visiting us and he asked if it would awaken Betty if he dictated answers to letters. I told him he could talk as he pleased and it would not bother her. I did not realize, however, that he would pace the floor as he dictated. As soon as he started walking back and forth, Betty woke up.

Betty was always the easiest of our five children to awaken. When Betty was a little girl, as soon as my feet hit the floor in the morning she would awake.

Sometime watch an entire TV program with the sound off. This will give you some conception of the deaf world.

2. *English words.* The American Sign Language did not originate in America but in France, so the first signs were for French words, not English. However, the deaf do not need to know French to learn the Sign Language. Signs are not for words, but for things. To English-speaking people, "mother" refers to the woman who bore us and cares for us. In French, "mere" refers to the woman who bore us and cares for us. "Madre" is the word used by Spanish-speaking people. Thus the open hand from the chin denotes "mother" to the deaf. Learn to think of the object and learn the sign for that object. Signs, like words, stand for things and events.

This is the way the deaf do it. Consequently, they think of you by an outstanding characteristic you may have—a large nose, ears, short hair, curls, etc.

There was a woman who helped at the Ranch during the summer for a number of years. She had unusually large protruding ears. So the deaf, when speaking of that woman, always signed. "Woman with big ears."

For a blind singer performing at the Ranch, they signed, "Blind B," for blind Billy.

148

Suggestions and Further Helps for Learning Sign Language

You will learn that the deaf often know a sign but not the English word for that sign. Betty, in talking to me one time, used the sign for "experienced." When I asked her what the sign was, she did not know the English word. It took me days to find out what she was trying to tell me—a certain person had experience.

3. *English sentences.* Learn to think and feel deaf. You do this by being with the deaf. A deaf boy may say, "I study school" for "I am going to school." This may be wrong English but it is not wrong signing. This is the language of the deaf. As one worker with the deaf put it, *"Be a conformist, not a reformer, in the use of this language."*

Ronnie, our foster deaf son, once said to me, "He is a *mean* preacher." He meant—"His preaching is too deep."

Sign Language is not a new way of saying the English language. It is a language all its own.

Don't Give Up

1. My husband often says, "If it were easy, everyone would be doing it." Determine in your heart not to give up. Just keep at it. Practice, associate with the deaf, and remember, Galatians 6:9 says, "Let us not be weary in well doing: for in due season we shall reap, if we faint not."

2. Do not let the deaf discourage you by arguing over which is the right sign. As long as you are learning signs, you should use the signs of the teacher. When you return home, take the signs of your locality. However, if each of your deaf have a different sign, make them take yours. Let them understand you know the correct way to sign the word.

3. Often Sign Language has no written form so it is not as uniform as we would like it to be. Often it is not taught to deaf children but is "just picked up." Consequently, some signs differ in various parts of the country.

4. Sign Language has been fairly well standardized. The language is uniform enough that we should be able to understand the deaf all around the world. Much can be accomplished via pantomime.

5. Deaf are very critical and plain spoken.

Example: A deaf man looking at a girl who had been away for several months said to her, "You were pretty when you were here before, but now you are ugly." Can you imagine a hearing man saying that to a young girl?

Sign Language for Everyone

The deaf are frank to tell you they don't like your hair or your dress. On the other hand, they are just as quick to tell you if they like something.

They feel no hesitation in asking your age, and then telling you how old you look!

6. Just remember, the deaf are desperate for interpreters and people to help them. And even though they criticize you, they will love you forever for your attempts to speak their language and to help them.

Recently my husband was in a certain city to preach and I went on the weekend to join him. When I walked into the church, a little old lady came running across the auditorium, grabbed me and hugged me. Then she signed, "Remember me? You came here a long time ago and told me about Jesus, and I was saved."

Years before, when I was just learning signs, we were in this same church. This lady came to church every service. I knew very little about interpreting, but I used what I knew and she was saved. How happy she was to see me and how she loved me for my feeble attempt to sign and tell her of Jesus!

7. Always remember, you cannot really get to know the language of signs in a class or from a book. A class and a book can only give you a start. To really learn the language you *must* associate with the deaf. Sign every chance you get. Watch them sign so you can grow more accustomed to their way of thinking.

8. Many signs are really just pictures. Learn to forget the English word and the sound of the word but remember how it looks and make the picture. Notice the following examples:

house	horse	deer	book	fence
town	cow	chicken	turtle	jail
boat	cat	chain	heaven	dish
telephone	hell	angel	door	road
airplane	lion	cross	crown	bridge

Signs that refer to clothing or object worn:

boy	girl	policeman	Indian	India
priest	poor	king	queen	boss

Signs that refer to size or degrees:

children	tall	fat	thin	large
small	tiny	much	few	more
improving	not improving			

Suggestions and Further Helps for Learning Sign Language

Signs that refer to actions, objects, or images associated with the word:

time	morning	night	church	hose
judge	hour	minute	devil	star
march	decision	bury	soldier	moon
day	meeting	funeral	hospital	sun

Signs that show something being done:

doctor	Baptist	monkey	bee	rain
nurse	Methodist	bear	snow	smell

Signs that show how an object is used or handled:

flower	bed	pie	candy	milk
baby	row	sheep	baseball	sugar
sew	banana	coffee	drive	butter
ice cream	cook	eggs	bread	

Signs that show feeling:

love	sick	wish	trouble	tired
happy	surprised	fear	doubt	good
satisfied	sad	excited	like	hate
bad	pity	lonesome	feel	angry
pain	funny	hungry	embarrassed	

Signs made by indication:

meet	follow	here	visit	serve
dream	come	below	where	carry
guide	you	go	above	move
wait	think	he	she	

Signs that show action:

run	leave	make	march	talk
play	walk	praise	work	bell
hurry	sing	practice	copy	draw
build	fight			

LESSON 10

Pronouns

Leave No Room for Doubt

1. Always remember: it is more important to be clear than to have speed. Because pronouns are used so often when speaking, it is good to spell he, his, him, her, they, etc. or use the name of the person the pronoun refers to in order to be sure the deaf know exactly of whom you are speaking.

Example: If we say, "Pete is riding his horse," the deaf can easily understand that "his" refers to Pete.

Oftentimes, however, by past conversation hearing people would know we meant Pete if we said, "He is riding his horse." But it should never be taken for granted that the deaf know. Always make sure by using the name. "Pete is riding his horse" is far better.

Often pronouns are used in hymns. But to be sure of clarity, Jesus, Christ, Lord (whichever fits best) should be used to make sure the deaf know of whom you are singing.

Example: "He lives, He lives, Christ Jesus lives today," would be better signed, "Jesus lives, Jesus lives, Christ Jesus lives today." Then it would be all right to continue, "He walks with me, etc."

2. When pointing to indicate "he," "she," "we," do not point if the person or object cannot be seen. Pointing can also refer to a thing or "it." Be sure what you are referring to is clearly visible so there will be no doubt of what or whom you are referring.

Example: If we were to sign, "They were here but they left in *it* (pointing to something outside) but when they return we will all ride the horses." Who are "they," what is "it," and who are "we"?

Example: "Bill and Pete were here. But they (spell) have gone to get the horses." Spell "they" because they are not present.

"Bill, here is Pete. You (point) both go to get the horses." You can point because they are present.

"This is my dress. It (point) is old but I like it (point)." You can point both times for "it" since the dress is right there.

"That was my dress on the clothesline. It (spell) was old so I left it (spell) home." Since the dress is not with you it is best to spell "it."

3. For possessive pronouns (my, mine, his, hers, theirs, ours) use the

open palm to show possession. Then clasp your hand to your chest (as a child might clasp something to himself) to show ownership.

4. "A" hand shows something done alone. It is used for "myself," "yourself," etc.

Examples:
   I fixed the stove myself.
   Get the candy yourself for the party.
   He did it for himself.
   She made the cake herself.

5. "er"—person sign—shows action being done.

speak-er	dream-er	bowl-er
think-er	farm-er	follow-er
teach-er	print-er	preach-er

   "ist"—also a way of showing a worker.
      type-ist   teeth-dentist (sign tooth-ist)

Prepositions

To

1. The sign for "to" is used properly only when movement is indicated.

Examples:

   We are going *to* the Bill Rice Ranch.
   I need *to* (omit) go *to* the office.
   We go *to* school on September 6.

2. If "for" can replace an infinitive then the "to" sign should not be used.

Examples:

   Julia came here (for) to find her father.
   They came here (for) to learn the signs.
   Bill will go to town (for) to buy meat.
   The father is here (for) to get the children.

3. Omit the "to" in an infinitive, and elsewhere, if it cannot be replaced by a preposition.

Examples:

> I want to (omit) go to the deaf class.
> I wish to (omit) stop (for) to get the apples.
> I went to (omit) town (for) to get my father.

On

1. The sign for "on" should be used only when "upon" could replace "on" in the sentence.

Examples:

> The flower is *on* the desk.
> Hang the picture *on* the wall.

2. Do not use the "on" sign in, "We are *on* time." We are not "upon" the time. It would be correct to sign, "We here right time."

In

1. Use the sign for "in" only when "into" could replace "in" in the sentence.

> Put the letter *in* the mail.
> He arrived in time for the fun. (Omit the "in.")
> Just in case you hear from her, let me know. (Change "just in case" to "if.")
> In the morning we will eat bacon. (Omit "in"—saying "morning time.")

Before

1. "Before" has different signs for different uses of the word.

Examples:

> It happened *before* I was born.
> John arrived *before* Tom.
> Marching on *before*.
> Jesus stood *before* Pilate.

2. The deaf do not use the "before" signs properly. But it is good for you to know them and try to cultivate the proper use for each "before."

Practice Sentences:

1. I arrived *before* the others.
2. It happened *before* I was born.

3. The man stood *before* the audience.
4. He sang *before* a crowd of one thousand.
5. I was here *before* he came.
6. The weather will change *before* night.
7. He went *before* the large group to lead them.

Articles

The, And, That

In speaking and writing English, we use words that are grammatically correct but actually unessential in conveying what we mean. For example: "The boy and the girl that came late lost the book and the pen." Leave out all the articles and the meaning is still clear. "Boy, girl came late lost book, pen."

Using "the," "and," and "that" sounds better to us but remember, the deaf have their own language. Signs are more tiring and time-consuming than speech, so the deaf, in spite of all we do, will leave out these nonessential words. If you sign every "the," "and," and "that," you find it becomes very tiresome to the signer as well as to the deaf person watching. A good rule is: Know the signs for "the," "and," and "that" but realize it is not necessary to use these signs as often you would say the words.

Practice Sentences:

What do you do with the pronouns, prepositions, and articles in the following sentences?

1. Shortly after *his* twelfth birthday, *he* began *to* grow faster.
2. Each time *he* tries *to* do better, *he* finds *he* is *the* same as *before.*
3. *He* never went *to the* beach *on* Friday again *and he* never went *in a* boat again.
4. *He* became deaf *in his* teens *and that* was *a* sad day for *him.*
5. *They* went *to* buy meat *to* make hamburgers *on* Friday.
6. *You* will like deaf people *in your* heart *and that* is *the* truth.
7. *I* did not know *you* were here *before* I came *to* town.
8. *He* changed *his* habits *before it* was *too* late.
9. *He* came *to* town *before his* father came.
10. Today *we* will answer *the* letter *that* came *and that* will be *the* one *on the* table.

LESSON 11

Tenses

In the English language we have words to express what has happened, what is happening right now, and what will happen in the future. In other words, we have *past, present,* and *future* tenses.

In dealing with tenses in the Sign Language, however, we will find some drastic changes from our English way of thinking. Deaf children are now being taught signs which indicate tense, but the adult deaf, for the most part, are not familiar with these signs.

Present Tense

Until recently, one sign has been used to express all the "to be" words: am, is, are, be, been, was, etc. This sign, made by placing the end of the index finger of the right hand beneath the lower lip, is also used for truth. (Truth is.)

Gallaudet College is now making an effort to make different signs for each word. Thus:

"A" beneath lip for "am."
"B" beneath lip for "be" or "been."
"I" beneath lip for "is."
"R" beneath lip for "are."

When speaking in the present, it is often good to use the "now" sign. This makes it clear that what you are speaking of is happening right now. Below are four correct ways to sign the same sentence using the "now" sign.

We (now) are going to church.
We are (now) going to church.
We are going to church (now).
(Now) We are going to church.

Future Tense

To show something will happen in the future, simply use the "future" sign or "will" sign.

Examples:

I can go (future) if you go some day soon.

We will feed the horses hay.
Our school will serve lunches.
I wish I could (future) go to Chicago.

Past Tense

As in the present and future, we do not have different signs for "was" and "were." Use the "past" sign or the "happened before" sign.

Examples:

John *was* here. John (past) here. John here (past).
He *was* here. He (past) here. He here (past).
They *were* here. They (past) here. They here (past).

In the English we may use the words "was" or "were" in a sentence more than once. In the language of signs, however, you need to use the sign only one time.

Examples: "I was at the Bill Rice Ranch and I was ready to ride a horse"—change to—"I (past) Bill Rice Ranch. I ready to ride horse." "We were in New York for three weeks and we were tired from so much walking"—change to—"We (past) visit New York three weeks; we very tired from walking."

Go, Gone, Went

1. For present action, sign, "We now go."
2. For future action, sign, "We will go," or "We go tomorrow."
3. For past action, sign, "We past gone," or "We finished go." If the action has just been completed, the "finished" sign is used in place of the "past" sign. If the time in the past needs to be definite, sign, "We go yesterday."

Notice: If you spell the verb to show correct tense, then you do not need to use the "now," "future," or "past" signs.

Have, Has, Had

These three words can be very troublesome in the Sign Language. The deaf think of the word "have" in terms of possession. They use the sign for have in this sense no matter how the word "have" is used. This, as in "before," is an example of how signs need to be taught properly to deaf children.

"Have" can have three different meanings:

"Have" as in "I have finished my work," or "I have finished eating my food."

"Have" as in "I have my work with me," or "I have a new car."

"Have" as in "I have to (must) finish my work," or "I have to (must) leave now."

Examples: "Have" as in finished. Use finish sign.

I have gone—I *finish* go.
I have eaten—I *finish* eat.
They have worked hard—They *finish* work hard.
He has learned signs—He *finish* learn signs.

In the finished *"have"* sign you may find you sometimes have the *"finished"* sign and then the *"have"* sign as in, "He *has had* his foot hurt." This would be signed, "He *finished have* his foot hurt." "When we *have learned* the lesson we will have an exam" sign, "When we *finish learn* lesson we will have exam."

Examples: "Have" as in possession.

I have a nice dog.
I have a new car.
We will have a good time.
The building has a red roof.
Come and have a good time with us.

I have a new baby.
We have a new teacher.
We had (past have) a good time.
The dog has a nice house.

Examples: "Have" as in must. Use the "must" sign in place of "have" sign.

I have to (must) hurry to town.
I have to (must) eat my vegetables.
I have to (must) sing tonight.
I have to (must) leave home.
I have to (must) get the food ready.
John and Bill have to (must) work for that man.
We have to (must) find the dog.

Practice Sentences

How do you sign the words in italics?

1. We *have* seen the Bill Rice Ranch.
2. John *will* go get the car but he *has* to eat first.

3. The cat *has* eaten his milk.
4. Bill *was* blamed for the mistake.
5. My father *was* a man who helped others.
6. They *have* a lot of money so they *can* help others.
7. The young man and young woman *will be* married on Friday.
8. The woman *was* very sick but she *had* a good doctor.
9. Who *has been* to town?
10. I *have* forgotten the story.

Possessives

1. The apostrophe "s" shows possession in English and also in signs. To make the apostrophe "s" make the "s" hand and twist it as if making an apostrophe.

Examples:

John's car. Spell John, then make apostrophe "s" sign.
Betty's mother. Spell Betty, then make apostrophe "s" sign.

2. Often in the Sign Language, the deaf take the French form of possession.

Examples:

Betty, her mother.
Bill, his money

3. In some sentences, it may be better to eliminate the apostrophe.

The ball's color—change to—The color of the ball.
The book's pages—change to—The pages of the book.

4. It is correct, as far as signing is concerned, to make the sign for a word and then add apostrophe "s."

Plurals

1. Make sure you leave no doubts about numbers or quantities when signing. For example, if the speaker said, "The men were here," and you signed, "The man was here," the deaf would have no way of knowing from your signs that there was more than one man. To sign this properly you would sign, "The man (two) were here," or "The man (many) were here."

2. The "many" sign or the number or quantity should be used with the noun to show more than one.

Example: The sign for children clearly tells us there are more than one. To be sure it is understood, however, you can sign "children" and then sign "four."

An example of signing to show quantity is "He needs more books." Getting "more" implies more than one.

3. The signs "many," "few," and "much" should be signed after a noun if the number or quantity is not clearly understood from the context of the sentence.

Practice Sentences

1. Betty *has* the baby boy—Kaye *has* the baby girl.
2. We *had* to go to church that night.
3. We *have* learned many new signs.
4. The *boy's* shoes *are* old.
5. I *would* like to buy the books but I *have* no money.
6. The book *has* many new words that I do not understand.
7. We *have been having* a lot of rain.
8. The dog *has to have* a new collar.
9. The *girl's* money *has been* lost.
10. They *have been* working on the camp to *have* it finished.

LESSON 12

"Do" Sign

There are five ways of using the "*do*" sign:

1. "Do" as in action. For this we use the "*do*" sign.

Examples:

He will *do* the job well (use sign for good).
She *did* the work several years ago.
We *did* that in a short time.

2. "Do" as used for emphasis. For this, spell "*do.*"

Examples:

I *do* hope you will hurry.
I *did* want to help him.
They *do* feel better today.

3. "Do" as in a question. Again, spell "*do.*"

Examples:

Do you know that girl?
Did he have some candy?
Do you like fried chicken?

4. "Do" as used in place of repeating the verb. Spell "*do.*"

Examples:

The girl signs as her friends *do.*
What does she think about what we *do?*
He can *do* the work that I *do.*

5. For the derivatives of "*do*"—does, did, done—use the "*5 finished*" hand.

Examples:

Are you *done* (*finished*) eating?
What have you *done?* (*finished*)
He has *done* (*finished*) his job.

"Not" Signs

There are two widely used signs for "not."

1. The sign most commonly used is the "A" hand. Put thumb under chin and flick it off. This sign is used for not, isn't, don't, doesn't, shouldn't, etc.

Examples:
I *don't* like that man.
It *isn't* right to fight with your brother.
We *shouldn't* count the money tonight.

2. The second "not" sign is made by spreading both hands apart, palms down, as if to say, "Cut it off" or "Don't blame me." Use this sign in such sentences as:
Don't do that.
Don't put the blame on me.
Pay attention to my words—*don't* look around.

Other Negative Signs

1. "Can't" is made by hitting right index finger against left index finger.
2. "Won't" is made by throwing right "A" hand back over right shoulder.
3. "No" is made by combining "N" and "O" into one gesture.
4. "None" is made by forming the letter "O" with both hands, then moving each hand away from the other to show there is nothing, zero. Besides using this sign for "none" it should sometimes be used when we say "no" or "aren't any" in such sentences as:

I have *no* money.
There were *no* people present.
I had *no* help.
There *aren't any* apples.

"Late" Sign

1. To indicate being behind time, use the "late" sign as in: "I am *late* for school.

2. The "late" sign can also be used to show that something has not arrived, as in: "The books have not arrived." You would sign this, "The books *late* arrived."

3. The deaf also use the "late" sign to express something that has not yet been accomplished. If you asked, "Have you ridden a horse?" the deaf might answer, "Late," meaning he has not gotten around to it yet.

4. "Late" is also used for the words "haven't," "hasn't," or "hadn't."

Examples:
    They haven't arrived—They *late* arrive.
    He hasn't finished the job—He *late* finish job.
    They hadn't heard Bill Rice—They *late* hear Bill Rice.

REMEMBER—use *"finish"* to show completion. Use *"late"* when not completed.

Examples for using *"finish"* or *"late"*:
    He has ridden—He *finish* riding.
    He hasn't ridden—He *late* ride.
    They haven't seen the animals—They *late* see animals.
    Bill has built the house—Bill *finish* build house.
    Bill hasn't built the house—Bill *late* build house.

"Same" Sign

There are two signs for the word "same."

1. One of these signs is made by placing two extended index fingers together, pointing away from self. When talking of two like-modeled cars, you would sign: "They (pointing to the cars) are the same (using the above-described "same" sign)." This sign is also used for "like," "too," "also," and "alike."

2. The other "same" sign is made with the "Y" hand. This sign is used when two people are alike in some way. If you were referring to a likeness between yourself and the person to whom you were talking, you would move the "Y" hand from yourself to that person. Often this sign is given after the sentence is signed. For example you would sign: "We both go to the Baptist church," then you would make the "same" sign using the "Y" hand.

Examples:
Using index fingers:
    The two cars are the *same.*
    He is not the *same* as his father.
    The twins look the *same.*

Using "Y" hand:
   We *both* have red dresses. (*Same.*)
   We *both* came from Texas. (*Same.*)
   He *agrees* with me now. (*Same.*)

Sizes of People and Things

1. People—To describe a person as either tall or short, raise or lower the hand to indicate height. For the descriptions of fat or thin, use a natural pantomime.

2. Things—To convey the idea that something is large, use the "L" hands before the sign for the object. Similarly, use cupped hands to indicate smallness. When describing large quantities, first cup the hands, then spread them apart—this is the sign for "much."

Examples:
   With all my love—With much (spread cupped hands apart) love.
   The small boy—A short (show height) boy.
   A large college—A ("L" hand) college.
   A little house—A (small cupped hands) house.

3. "Little bit"—Another sign to describe size or amount is made by flicking the thumb off the index finger.

Examples:
   I would like just a *little* food.
   He makes just a *little* money.
   He had only a *little* help.

INDEX

Index

Index

Instructions for Counting

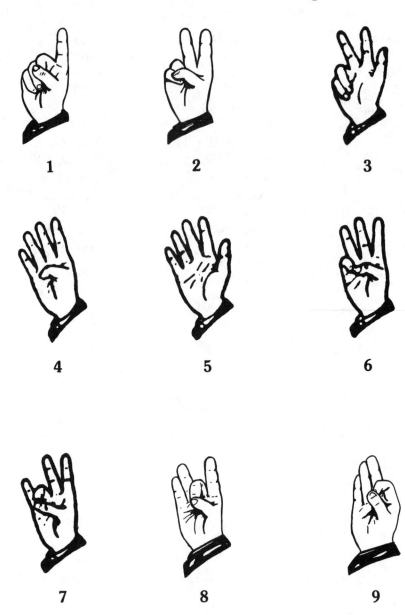